OBADIAH AND HAGGAI

Readings: A New Biblical Commentary

OBADIAH AND HAGGAI

Graham S. Ogden

Sheffield Phoenix Press
2022

Copyright © 2022 Sheffield Phoenix Press
Published by Sheffield Phoenix Press
University of Sheffield, S10 2TN

www.sheffieldphoenix.com

All rights reserved.
No part of this publication may be reproduced or transmitted in any form or by any means, electronic or mechanical, including photocopying, recording or any information storage or retrieval system, without the publisher's permission in writing.

A CIP catalogue record for this book
is available from the British Library

Typeset by the HK Scriptorium

ISBN: 978-1-914490-09-5 (HB)
ISBN: 978-1-914490-10-1 (PB)

Contents

Abbreviations	ix
Preface	xi

OBADIAH

Introduction	3
Outline	3
Contents	3
On Reading Obadiah	4
Authorship and Unity	5
Date	6
Oral Transmission	7
Prophetic Language?	8
Oracles against Foreign Nations	9
The Day of the Lord	9
Obadiah's Theological Perspective	10
Exegesis	11
Verse 1a Title	11
Verses 1b-4 A Message concerning Edom	12
Verses 5-7 Edom's Allies Prove Treacherous	16
Verses 8-10 Edom's Wisdom and Power Destroyed	18
Verse 11 The Core Charge against Edom	19
Verses 12-14 Edom's Treachery Described	20
Verses 15-18 Edomite Treachery to Be Repaid.	22
Verses 19-21 Edom Dispossessed	25
Postscript	28
Obadiah and Deuteronomy	28
Obadiah and Psalm 137	29
Fulfilment?	29
A Conclusion	29
Brief Bibliography	31

HAGGAI

Introduction	35
From Little Things Big Things Grow	35
On Reading Haggai	36
Haggai and Israel's Prophetic Tradition	39
Haggai in Historical Context	41
The Prophet Haggai	43
On Haggai, Zerubbabel and Joshua	44
Aramaic or Hebrew?	46
Prophetic Insight	47
Literary Features of Haggai	49
Haggai and Deuteronomy	51
Authorship	53
Dating Haggai	54
Haggai and its Theological Ideas	55
Haggai 1	60
Outline of Contents	60
Structure	60
1.1-15a First Dated Message	61
1.1-2 The Editor's Introduction	64
1.3-11 Call to Rebuild the Temple	71
1.5-6 'Consider . . .' I	75
1.7-11 'Consider . . .' II	77
1.12-15a The People Respond	82
Haggai 2	87
1.15b—2.9 Second Dated Message	87
1.15b–2.1 Second Message: October 17, 520 BCE	89
2.10-19 Third Message: December 18, 520 BCE	99
2.10-14 A Priestly Ruling on Holiness and Haggai's Application	101
2.15-19 Two Calls to Reflect on the Future	106
2.18-19 'Consider . . .' IV	111
2.20-23 Fourth Message: December 18, 520 BCE	113
Postscript	119
Haggai and the Modern Reader	119
On Being Chosen	120
On God and Nature	121

God and the Nations	122
On Prophecy	123
Theological Exclusivism	124
Analogical Application	125
Conclusion	127
Appendix A	129
Haggai and Prophetic Forms	129
Select Bibliography	131

Abbreviations

AB	Anchor Bible
BT	*Bible Translator*
DH	Deuteronomistic History
JOTT	*Journal of Translation and Textlinguistics*
LXX	Septuagint
MT	Masoretic Text
NCBC	New Century Bible Commentary
NICOT	New International Commentary on the Old Testament
NRSV	New Revised Standard Version
OTL	Old Testament Library
TDOT	*Theological Dictionary of the Old Testament.* Edited by G.J. Botterweck and H. Ringgren
WBC	Word Biblical Commentary
UBS	United Bible Societies
ZAW	*Zeitschrift für die alttestamentliche Wissenschaft*

Preface

Many years ago I had the great privilege of studying under the late B.W. 'Barney' Anderson. One of the most memorable pearls of wisdom that he repeated often with students was 'Read the text. You will be amazed at how much light it sheds on the commentaries!' It is advice that so frequently comes to mind, and none more so than when asked to offer a commentary in the Sheffield Phoenix Readings series. Where does one begin when thinking of writing a commentary if not with hours spent working closely with the Hebrew text.

For the past 12 years I have been heavily involved in preparing notes on the Minor Prophets for a new Study Bible Project, and it just so happened that I had been working on them when the offer came to write. There were rhetorical elements in Obadiah that seemed to me to be quite important markers. The title of the document, identifying it as a vision, seemed not to fit the content that followed, and relevant to both form and content was a determination of the verbal forms as prophetic or volitional. In Haggai, both in the text and in what I saw as background to the text, there were elements that intrigued me—seeming non-sequiturs, truncated narrative, repetitions, and hyperbole. On these matters, commentators' notes were not always as helpful as I had hoped and expected.

It is very easy for readers of commentaries to get lost in the mass of technical details of footnotes, multiple references to scholarly works, and critiques of scholarly positions taken, but often no satisfying answers to some of the questions one has arising from the Hebrew text. Of course, there may not be answers to some of the questions one asks, whether textual, historical, literary or theological, and one should respect the limitations that the text itself imposes.

The commentary that follows will seek to identify the main ideas and questions that seem to this writer to emerge from a close reading of the text of Obadiah and Haggai, with only marginal reference to the views of the academic community; it is my reading of the text of these two short but important documents from the early postexilic Jewish community in Jerusalem.

I am deeply grateful to Sheffield Phoenix Press for the opportunity to offer the commentaries for wider discussion.

I wish to acknowledge that some early draft materials have benefitted from comments by some of my United Bible Society translation colleagues, but I do need to mention Dr. Nigel Statham in particular.

I need to acknowledge that the perspective taken, and the views expressed are nonetheless those of this now ancient reader.

OBADIAH

A Commentary

Introduction

The document known as Obadiah's Vision (Heb. *ḥᵃzôn-'obadyāh*), the smallest document to be included in the Scroll of the Twelve, is generally assumed to be a 'prophetic' work. Its inclusion along with other prophetic books in the Scroll of the Twelve lends credence to this assumption, but there is little in the book itself that makes that designation obvious. And if one considers Jonah, the following book in the Scroll sequence, a narrative created *about* a prophet and not a prophetic pronouncement, then there is justification for a broader view of Obadiah as 'prophet' within this collection. Yes, Obadiah shares material with Jeremiah 49 and exhibits a similar attitude toward the deceitful actions of foreign enemies noted in other prophetic books such as Joel and Amos, but it also shares in the emotion-laden anti-Edom outburst seen in Psalm 137, which is clearly not 'prophetic'. So, what kind of literary work is Obadiah? Is Obadiah really a prophetic text or a statement condemning Edom and the nations for past actions? While much of the text looks back to Edom's involvement with the Babylonian invasion in 587 BCE, vv. 15-21 do have an eye to the future, threatening revenge, but it is presented as a call for imminent revenge against all the nations involved, and against Edom in particular.

Outline

1a	Title
1b-4	A Message Concerning Edom
5-7	Edom's Allies Prove Treacherous
8-10	Edom's Wisdom and Power Destroyed
11	Edom's Treachery Defined
12-14	Edom's Treachery Described
15-18	Treachery to Be Repaid
19-21	Dispossessing Edom

Contents

The above outline coincides with a range of Obadiah's rhetorical features, the most obvious being brackets or couplets of phrases, of themes built around a central core verse, v. 11. This v. 11 is the numerically central verse in a collection of sayings, summarizing the preceding ten verses and introducing the following ten. It is a clever construction device that is found in some other prophetic works, e.g. Joel 2.17, around which an editor has arranged a whole work. Obadiah's main rhetorical features are:

Verses 1b-4 are a unit set within the messenger form, 'Thus says the Lord . . . , says the Lord', in which 'bring down' is the climactic verb.

Verses 5-7 have a duo of conditional clauses featuring (a) 'if . . . , would they not . . . ?' and (b) an exclamatory 'how . . . !' in vv. 5-6 and concluding in v. 7 with the charge of Edomite stupidity.

Verses 12-14 consist of a series of eight negative imperatives with the fixed form: 'you should not have . . . on the day of . . .'

Verses 15-16 present two parallel result clauses: '(for) as you have . . . , so may you . . .'

Verses 17-18 focus on Zion, Jacob, Joseph, who 'escape' and on Esau, who does 'not escape'. People are referred to using the keyword 'house'.

Verses 19-21 build around a clutch of regional geographical references or tribal enemies who will dispossess Edom, with v. 21 and the 'saved' as the climax.

The reading being proposed gives priority to these rhetorical features in terms of both the document's structure and its purpose or function.

On Reading Obadiah

The particularity of a document like Obadiah demands that readers make every effort to consider it within its literary and historical contexts. In this case, the obvious connections with other prophetic works and with Psalm 137 suggest that Obadiah needs to be approached as one component in the wide body of evidence of Judaean response to the post-587 BCE trauma. Late additions to Jeremiah 49, Joel 3 and Amos 9, along with the highly emotional outburst reflected in the exilic Psalm 137, point to a setting for Obadiah in which Edom's participation in Judah's demise remained a most painful memory for a great many years, from soon after the event through to a possible early fifth-century date. Throughout this time, Edom's treachery was not to be forgotten, so it remained a matter of intense resentment at the level expressed in Ps. 137.7-9.

The reading of Obadiah being proposed will acknowledge those feelings of anger and resentment, and read the Obadiah document in that light, as evidence of wide-ranging expressions of anger calling for revenge on Edom, rather than as a 'prophetic' pronouncement about what will happen to it.

The principle guiding this reading of Obadiah is that the text has been brought together by an unnamed editor drawing on the oral material that focused on the fateful events of 587 BCE. That material was widespread, as is evidenced by the fact that several other OT books have also drawn on it and based their messages in whole or in part on it. It was a body of oral material that lamented and expressed anger at what had happened to Jerusalem and its Temple in particular but that had also called into question its view of Yahweh and his unique relationship with Israel. The resentment expressed in Ps. 137.7-9 catches most vividly the mood of the people, and here in Obadiah we can see another dimension of that as the people called for revenge.

Authorship and Unity

Scholars are divided on the question of the authorship and unity of this brief 21-verse document. Such a situation is inevitable given that the document is the end result of a lengthy period of oral transmission during which diverse material and differing versions of responses to Edom's treachery found expression. That the document is attributed to one individual (assumed), Obadiah, of whom nothing but his name is known, depends entirely on the heading or title provided by the final editor. Whether the name Obadiah was that of a real person or more of a title—'a servant of the Lord'—it was the final editor who is credited with collating the material and adding its title—Obadiah's Vision. That anonymous editor, the real author of this final product, has linked the material to Obadiah and designed the structure of the work, building it around the numerically central v. 11.

Obadiah the document is a literary construction with a unity of theme throughout, namely Edom's treachery and its aftermath, and the structure provided by the editor concentrates that focus. However, the materials themselves are rhetorically diverse, and the syntax complex, with singular and plural verb forms, second-person and third-person references all combined within the one statement, and Jerusalem referred to in the first-person as 'my sacred mountain'. This latter appears to suggest that God is speaker. See vv. 15-18 notes.

Apart from the initial vv. 1c-4 and the use of the messenger form to contain its message, there is little in the remaining verses that carry the sense that Obadiah spoke of what the editor has named as his 'vision'. What did Obadiah see? This raises the question of why it was given such a title. The collection throughout uses mainly third-person narrative, describing the actions of the Edomites and the nations and accusing them of terrible deeds done against Jerusalem in the past.

A further editorial factor at work overall is also visible in the way that sections are tied together. For example, vv. 8-10 are linked to the preceding v. 7 summary by means of the repeated noun *tᵉbûnâ*, 'understanding', further explaining how unwise or foolish Edom had become. Similarly, vv. 19-21 are linked together by the theme verb *yāraš* relating to Edom's dispossession. The most striking rhetorical feature, however, is the series of eight negative imperative forms in vv. 12-14, along with the phrase 'on the day of', referring variously to Jerusalem being attacked.

Additionally, as is a feature in the Scroll's sequencing of the Minor Prophets as a whole, Obadiah's opening verse has been linked directly to the close of the preceding book, Amos 9.12, via the repetition of 'Edom' and 'the nations'. (See also the similar rhetorical link between Joel 3.16 and Amos 1.2.)

Past scholarship has suggested that some material in this final version of Obadiah may, on the basis of representing a different theme, be from a later editorial hand. This has resulted in some arguing that v. 15a and vv. 16-21 do not belong to the original draft but have been added later in a further editing procedure. Others have sought close examination of the strophic or poetic rhythm of the verses and concluded that v. 15b should follow v. 14, and that v. 21 should follow v. 17. Interesting though these suggestions for re-ordering the text might be, they arise from a reader's personal evaluation and not from hard textual evidence.

Overall then, Obadiah the document stands as the result of a careful and extended editorial process bringing together various rhetorical components in the oral materials circulating post-587 that gave voice to Judaeans' longing for revenge against its 'brother' Edomite community.

Date

No date has been provided by the editor; no connection is made with any contemporary event or situation. In this matter, Obadiah joins the ranks of other undated works—Jonah, Nahum, Habakkuk and Malachi. Obadiah is not tied to any one brief moment nor perhaps to any one individual; rather it collates related material from a broad postexilic period.

From the very moment Jerusalem was attacked by the Babylonians in 587 BCE, aided by the arrogant and opportunistic Edomites, Judaeans were furious with their sometimes friendly but contentious neighbour. The tradition that Edomites were descended from Esau meant that this act of treachery was seen as an outworking of the old enmity between Jacob and Esau (Gen. 27.30-45), making the pain of Edomite treachery all the more intolerable. That bitter anger with regard to Edomite deception and its participation in the attack on Jerusalem tainted Judaean attitudes toward Edom for at least the next century if Obadiah is dated, as it is by some, to 450 BCE. However, given the nature of Obadiah as a collection of oral responses to Edom and the nations over an extended period, a specific date for this final form of Obadiah cannot be determined. Material shared by Obadiah, Jeremiah 49, Joel, Amos and Psalm 137 can cover a wide period post-587 and so does not provide sufficient clear evidence allowing a date to be specified.

This means that readers may locate Obadiah from any moment within the period of the Babylonian exile to some time after having returned to Jerusalem under Persian control with permission to rebuild, i.e. from 586 to c. 500 BCE. More precise dating is not possible.

Oral Transmission

When investigating the prophetic materials, it is appropriate to presume an extended period in which the prophetic messages were repeated, were handed on, and in many cases reshaped, supplemented, developing updated versions of the basic outline and structure. Eventually an editing or redaction process gathered the oral material in its multiform versions, and it became 'frozen' in one or more written forms. The process is obviously complicated and can range over a long period of time—consider the book of Isaiah with two hundred years of history before it assumes its final 66-chapter shape.

Obadiah likewise reflects a period of oral transmission about which one can know very little other than that components show its close relationship with material found also in Jeremiah 49, Amos 9.12, Joel 2.32; 3.19-21 and Psalm 137. It is the almost word-for-word identification with parts of Jer. 49.7-16 that attracts most attention, along with close links with the language of Joel. Difficulties in fixing a specific date for these late-exilic to early postexilic materials means that one cannot confidently trace lines of influence from one to the other. On the other hand, to assume that one body of text has borrowed from or been heavily influenced by another and earlier text is not always justified. It is equally possible that, as happens in an oral world, phrases and other rhetorical devices do arise and spread rapidly through a community, establishing themselves as fixed forms that are widely shared and used by multiple authors or editors.

The wide spread of fixed forms in the case of anti-Edomite rhetoric points to what had become a pervasive manner of speaking of the events of 587 BCE. An oral tradition had grown up around the Edomite issue, and the whole of Judaean society thereafter expressed its overwhelming anger at Edom via these established sayings and images. Obadiah is just one such iteration.

As with all oral transmission, variations in the details of a communication make their way into the process. It has to be expected that one version of a text relating to an event or incident may differ from another; full verbal or rhetorical consistency across the oral event is illusory. For this reason, 'correcting' Obadiah's text where it varies from that in Jeremiah 49, as some have suggested, is completely unjustified.

Prophetic Language?

One of the issues that must be addressed in reading Obadiah is the way in which the Hebrew verbs employed are to be regarded. Since Hebrew verbs are indicative of 'state'—completed or incomplete/repetitive actions—their time reference is dependent on the overall context or surrounding supplementary linguistic forms. The question raised in Obadiah's use of the verbs is whether perfective forms denoting completed activity are what some want to call 'prophetic perfects', verbs that identify matters God has already determined even though they are yet to be realized, or are they simply relating past completed events? Are the imperfect verb forms and their equivalents promises of future action, or are they volitional forms calling for Edom and the nations to be punished?

If one believes the text to be prophetic, it would be logical to regard a future-oriented rendering as appropriate. Most translations follow that logic, using declarative future tenses to render the verbs, but there is no absolute reason for such a view. Reference to the day of the Lord as 'near' or imminent in v. 15 calls for divine judgment to fall on Edom in the here and now, not in some vague future. Obadiah 15-16, which speak of the nations who are guilty of all the despicable actions listed in vv. 12-14, things that should not have been done, have the form *yēʿāseh* (imperfective), which can be read as jussive, 'let it be done (to you)'. Similarly, for those who in v. 16 'drank' on the sacred mountain, the verb form *yištû* (imperfective) can be read as the jussive 'let them drink' or 'may they drink', expressing a deep longing or hope that the nations will suffer for the attack on Jerusalem. Malediction and angry outbursts against the nations seem to be intended in this section. In fact, each of the imperfective verbs in this section, vv. 15-18, not only can be viewed as volitional; this is surely their intention rather than being declarations of some vague future possibility. It is from this viewpoint that the present commentary is written.

Further justification for reading the imperfective verbs as jussive can be found in the close relationship between Obadiah and the anti-Edom sentiments expressed in Psalm 137. Both Obadiah and the psalm belong to the body of material that gave expression to the post-587 BCE bitter resentment that Judaeans felt toward Edom. The jussive verb forms in Ps. 137.5-6 pour out resentment and call for justice to be meted out upon Edom, and this same form is used in Obad. 15-16. Rather than prophetic predictions, the sentiments expressed throughout Obadiah are for the nations, especially Edom, to be dispossessed, and for Jerusalem to be restored to its place as the Lord's domain. It is this perspective on the text overall that suggests that the Obadiah document is not 'prophetic' in the more traditional sense, but rather a collection of sayings that gives expression to Judaean longing to see Edom and the nations suffer for what they had done. Whether there lies behind this document some kind of formal liturgical activity may be considered, but no specific evidence remains apart from the community voice in Psalm 137.

The translation provided in this commentary is my own and reflects the verb use as jussives similar to that found in Ps. 137.7-9.

Oracles against Foreign Nations

Israel's oracles against foreign powers were an important feature of some prophetic collections. Isaiah 15–23, Jeremiah 46–50, Amos 1–2, in particular, pronounced judgment on their enemies. These foreign nations were not themselves the intended recipients or direct objects of these verbal attacks; the messages were only for the prophets' domestic audiences, and heard only by them. They served to express a longing for a better future for Judah, even if exaggerated, as well as being a vehicle for raging at the power of the enemy and its god. Obadiah's vision, so called, gathers many of what were the current oral outbursts against Edom being vented over this extended period of time—perhaps from 580 to 500 BCE. The rhetoric as such was not created by Obadiah but was an example of a shared body of poetic speech directed against the nations, and against Edomites in particular. The devastation of Jerusalem in 587 BCE by the Babylonian army was a reality, and for the Deuteronomic cohort was accepted as God's judgment on Judah's religious failures, especially that of King Manasseh. However, this fact was now far less important than was Edomite treachery, their troops having joined the Babylonian attack on Judah in 587 BCE. In this later period, Babylon was no longer the main enemy; treacherous Edom was.

The Day of the Lord

The concept of the 'Day' or 'Day of the Lord', which often refers to some unspecified future moment, is used in different senses in Obadiah. In v. 8 the 'Day' appears on the surface to refer to some moment in the future (but see below for discussion), while in vv. 11-14, where the majority of examples occur, the reference is clearly to the past, to the time or occasion on which Jerusalem was attacked, as in Ps. 137.7. In v. 15 the 'Day' is a moment of imminent divine judgment—it is 'near'– meaning that moment has essentially arrived; Judah wants to see the punishment carried out in the here and now, not in some far-distant moment. The verbs in this section, vv. 15-18, are to be read as jussives, as Judah calls for the nations to be dealt with in the same manner as they had dealt with it.

Obadiah's Theological Perspective

The theological view(s) resident within the Obadiah document are not front and centre; they lie under or behind the call for justice meted on the Edomites and nations who participated in the 587 BCE attack on Judah and its capital. The editor has included three first-person references, suggesting that it is the Lord speaking (e.g. vv. 4, 8, 16); otherwise the narrative is set as third-person report and focused on the call for divine punishment, as in v. 15.

God is assumed to have a special relationship with Judaeans, one that meant that God will act in their interests over that of others. The terms of the Davidic covenant (2 Sam. 7) assured them that God was on their side in perpetuity. Israel believed that its God, Yahweh, resident in Zion, was nevertheless active throughout the world to both reward and punish, to save and destroy. They could therefore appeal to God for action on their behalf. Implicit in this appeal is the notion of Holy War, that Israel's God goes ahead of the armies to defeat the enemy, for the enemy of Israel is the enemy of its God.

Readers familiar with the prophetic literature more generally will be surprised that Obadiah makes no mention of sin and rebellion, a theme that dominates the concerns of other prophetic books. Despite the brevity of Obadiah and its focus on Edom, it is surprising that here sin is ignored and thus calls for national repentance absent.

Furthermore, the editor believes that his God, being just, is the one who ensures justice is done among the nations, but in this context it is a view that raises a significant problem. According to the Deuteronomic record (2 Kgs 24), the attack on Judah/Jerusalem was itself a divine judgment on Judah's evil ways, a point that Obadiah quietly ignores, so it is more than ironic that he would call for action against those nations who were party to that earlier divine intervention. For Obadiah's editor, God obviously is on his side—a purely nationalistic or tribal perspective on the divine.

Exegesis

Verse 1a Title

The editor has set the title of the document as a report of Obadiah's vision. The Hebrew *ḥᵃzôn*, 'vision', is recognized as being of Aramaic origin, so borrowed into Hebrew during the period of the Babylonian exile some time after 587 BCE. The root word does describe something as 'seen', and is often associated with the more generic *rā'â,* 'see', linked to the prophetic visionary experience, whether figurative or concrete. It has been argued that the verb *ḥāzâ* relates specifically to 'a nocturnal perception of a divine voice during a deep sleep' (Jepsen), though not in the same category as a dream. On the other hand, there was no guarantee that what a prophet claims to have seen (*ḥāzâ*) was not a lie (Jer. 14.14; 23.16; Ezek. 12.21-27). Why the editor chose that title is unexplained, as is its field of reference.

The notion of a 'vision', whether physically viewed or more imagined, is a private matter for the person concerned and an experience of which others may need convincing. While the prophets do not seem to have used the term *ḥᵃzôn* to refer to their own experience or to their message, it is the redactors who do make use of it, as in Isa. 1.1; 13.1; Amos 1.1; Mic. 1.1, and here in Obadiah. It has become a technical term, a neologism that came into use from the exilic period. As a term of foreign origin, the precise meaning in its new context is problematic. What the 'content' of Obadiah's vision was is difficult to ascertain since the following material is entirely narrative without reference to any visual content. This makes the *ḥᵃzôn* term so ambiguous as to render it unhelpful; claims as to its semantic value and implied divine origin are questionable. If the title is the only evidence that Obadiah has potential as a 'prophetic' text, given that there is no further reference to anything visual in the next 20 verses, then one may wonder why it was incorporated into the Scroll of the Twelve rather than placed elsewhere.

Little is known about 'Obadiah'. Whether it is an individual's given name, or that person's role, male or female, is unclear. The name is descriptive of a role, namely a 'Servant of Yah'. The *yāh* ending is found in numerous Hebrew names, e.g. Zechariah (*zᵉkaryāh*), and Gedaliah (*gᵉdalyāh*), or the longer *yāhû* form as in Jeremiah (*yirmᵉyāhû*) and Josiah (*yō'šîyāhû*), and in *halᵉlû-yāh*, 'praise the Lord'. Scholars are divided as to whether *yāh* is a shortened form of *yāhû* and connected to the better-known divine name YHWH, generally referred to as Yahweh. Others contend that a divine name would not be shortened. Many assume that the three forms all relate to the same divine being with the shorter *yāh*-form generally found only in poetry.

Verses 1b-4 A Message concerning Edom

Thus says the Lord God concerning Edom:
'We have heard a report from the Lord, and a messenger has been sent among the nations: "Rise up! Let us rise against it for battle!"
2 Look, I have made you least among the nations; you are utterly despised.
3 Your proud heart has deceived you, you that live in the clefts of the rock, whose dwelling is in the heights.
You say in your heart, "None can bring me down to the ground?"
4 Though you soar aloft like the eagle, though your nest is set among the stars, from there I can bring you down,'
    says the Lord.

The initial vv. 1b-4, set within a messenger form, suggest that this is in fact a prophetic work and worthy of inclusion in the Scroll of the Twelve, though there is no point at which Obadiah is specifically identified as a prophet. Whether this document is actually 'prophetic' is a question that needs to be asked. And, as noted above, the inclusion of this document in the Scroll alongside the Jonah story points to the need for a broader definition of the noun 'prophet' within this collection. This writer will argue that rather than Obadiah being a collection of future-oriented prophetic statements, its content is more in the nature of angry outbursts expressing a Judaean longing for Edom to suffer, to be taken down, together with celebrating its inevitable humiliation.

Apart from the title assigned to the work, the editor has provided a standard formal opening with 'Thus says the Lord God (*'ᵃdonây yhwh)*', adding the intended object of that word as 'to/for/concerning Edom'. This formulaic opening was not part of an original message but is an editor's introduction to his report that follows. Only then does the reader in v. 2 come to what Obadiah is reported as saying, literally, 'A hearing we have heard from the Lord'. That introduction is brought to a conclusion in v. 4 with the formal 'says the Lord', thus formally bracketing vv. 1c-4. The final statement in this section is the first-person assertion that God can bring down the Edomites from their stronghold. Edom's arrogance and belief in its invincibility is the focus, with the climax in a play on the verb 'bring down' in vv. 3-4. What Edom regards as an impossibility is assuredly not so!

There is a high degree of rhetorical overlap between Obad. 2-4 and Jer. 49.14-16. Some commentators have assumed that Obadiah has copied Jeremiah, arguing on the assumption that Jeremiah 49 predates Obadiah. In the process, the claim is that Obadiah has modified that text slightly; it is an assumption that cannot be validated. There has been no copying, for each offers a slightly differing version of some of the oral material in circulation that dealt with the painful issue of Edom's deceit in joining Babylonian troops when Jerusalem was sacked in 587 BCE.

The first detail to note is that the Obadiah text uses a first-person plural verb 'we have heard'—Jer. 49.14 uses a singular—but the 'we' is not identified in any manner. Following on directly from the the editor's introductory form 'Thus says the Lord God' one could be forgiven for thinking that the speaker 'we' is God. There is a disjunction between this and the content of vv. 1b-4 and the messenger form that surrounds it. Presumably 'we' refers to the Judaean community as a whole, for it certainly does not involve Obadiah as spokesperson conveying a message to his community; it is a dispassionate report of something he and others have heard, not something he has seen—so why the title Obadiah's Vision?

The second detail to note is that the content of vv. 1b-4, using Hebrew perfect verbs, refers back to Edom's activities. It reviews and challenges Edom's pride and sense of security. Reading the verbs as 'prophetic perfects' and the passage as future oriented has been one way of reading this text, but it needs questioning. The reading plan being offered in this commentary views the verbs as referring to Edom's past actions as a kind of summary of the issue against which the Judaeans are railing.

The object of the verb 'heard' is emphasized by being placed ahead of the verb and is literally 'that which was heard', or, a report. That report was carried to the nations by one identified only as a 'messenger', while the one sending the messenger is not identified; it is clearly not Obadiah as either the sender or the one sent. However, the report to the nations is in the form of an imperative, a call to which the 'we' responded with 'let us arise and (go) against her for battle'. There is a similar call in Jer. 49.28 to 'Arise and go against (Hazor)', repeated in Jer. 49.31, suggesting that this kind of call is an element in a trope relating to announcements involving foreign peoples, although the call to 'arise' itself is a frequent prelude to all pleas for divine action. Much in this opening scene is recorded in vague and nonspecific language as one would expect of an editor applying a generic form to the material.

The Jer. 49.14 text also adds a call not found in Obadiah, namely 'gather yourselves together', to embrace the nations in the call to arms against Edom. Who is included in that call is likewise unclear.

2 'Look, I have made you a small thing among the nations, you have been utterly despised.'

Verse 2 essentially mimics Jer. 49.15 but lacking the initial *kî*, 'for', that introduces a reason for attacking Edom, unless *kî* serves as the emphatic 'indeed'. Both texts regard the demeaning of Edom as bringing it international shame, with the Jeremiah version adding all humanity as witness to that, while Obadiah chooses to emphasize the great degree of shame. The wording here is clearly intended to demean Edom as a small and insignificant entity within the wider family of nations.

It is the verb used (Heb. *n^etattîkā*) that is at issue—is it a so-called 'prophetic perfect', meaning 'I will make you', a future action already determined by God but yet to be realized, or is it a simple statement of fact, 'I have made/appointed you'? Commentators who see this document as prophetic generally favour the former view. However, the perfective form of the verb is making a clear statement—Edom was in fact a minnow among the nations of the day; it is not a status that lies in its future. The pronoun object 'you' needs clarification; most read it as a divine declaration in which 'you' refers to Edom, who is internationally shamed. The use of first-person address does imply God as speaker, yet the overall content of the report does not otherwise indicate that this is a divine speech but rather is editorial reporting of what was heard (v. 1).

Verses 3-4 obviously relate to Jer. 49.16, but the degree of shared form and vocabulary points to each text being a distinct version of what can be supposed as an original message. Deception, arrogance and the metaphor of the eagle are all common ideas, but the slight variations indicate that they are not copied by either editor; rather, each is an independent version of the status of Edom. The important climactic verb, 'bring down', is central to both, as it is to the same message repeated in Amos 9.2.

3 'Your proud heart has deceived you, you that live in the clefts of the rock, whose dwelling is in the heights. You say in your heart, "Who can bring me down to the ground?"'
4 'Though you soar like the eagle, though your nest is set among the stars, from there I can bring you down', says the Lord.

Jeremiah 49.16: The terror you inspire and the pride of your heart have deceived you, you who live in the clefts of the rock, who hold the height of the hill,.

Although you make your nest as high as <u>the eagle's, from there I will bring you down, says the Lord</u>.

Both Obadiah and the parallel texts affirm Edom's arrogance and sense of invincibility, its belief that it will never be 'brought down'. The rhetorical question form used in Obad. 3c, 'Who can bring me down?' are imagined words put into the mouth of a typical Edomite. They deny that such is a possibility, a direct challenge to anyone, including God, thinking to bring about Edom's defeat and humiliation. There is a possible play in v. 3 with the Hebrew noun *sela'*, 'rock', doubling as representing Edom (see 2 Kgs 14.7). This is the only potential reference to Edom in this opening section aside from the editorial introduction.

Presenting Edom in these terms reflects the geographical reality of the Edomite territory to the east of the Dead Sea. The mountains on that side of the Jordan rift valley rise to 5,700 metres, much higher than the hills of its western side (c. 3,000 metres). Its deep ravines are cut by rivers such as the Arnon, which become raging torrents after the heavy storms that can lash the heights but leave the western side barren and dry, the rain-shadow area. Edom was a challenge to all enemies because of its natural defences.

Verse 4 features paired Hebrew phrases preceded by the particle *'im*, '(even) if' or 'though'. They both speak of possible or contingent situations. While Jer. 49.16 uses the alternative particle *kî*, *'im* is prominent in the Amos 9.2-4 version, where remote hiding places and mountain tops are similarly identified, claiming that 'even from there I can bring you down'. The particles are followed by imperfective verbs to express timeless contingencies, not some planned future time; they assert the fact that Edom can always be 'brought down'.

The section concludes with the second element in the messenger form, 'says the Lord', closing off the first rhetorical unit. The intention for this unit seems to be to present the speech as a divine address by enclosing it within a traditional form. This move by the editor would make sense in the context of its inclusion within the prophetic collection of the Scroll of the Twelve. However, there is only one other context in which first-person reference to God is found (v. 8), all other potential references to God being in third-person narrative comments. The overall impression is that the editor has brought together disparate materials circulating in the Judaean community that express its attitude toward Edom.

The message contained within this initial frame concerns Edom and the nations. However, it is not addressed to them, nor is it something the Edomites will hear, for its function is to give expression to anti-Edomite feelings within Judaea. Who would bring down Edom? Certainly not the

Judaeans, despite the rallying call of v. 1c. And which of the nations is going to rise against Edom on Judaea's behalf? The section reflects Judaean anger with Edom's betrayal and its longing for revenge as they call on God to wage Holy War on their behalf.

In these first verses, the materials shared by Obadiah and Jer. 49.14-16 are clearly visible; the theme and wording are largely common, though variations are also obvious. However, with Obad. 5 the comparable text changes to that of Jer. 49.9, another independent but common illustration.

Verses 5-7 Edom's Allies Prove Treacherous

This section begins with two conditional clauses presenting potential situations; they are in the form of rhetorical questions anticipating a negative response. Their structure is distinctive: 'If (*'im*) ... X came to you ... would they not ($h^a l\hat{o}$') ... ?' (5a,c). There are also two statements introduced by the exclamatory 'how (*'eyk*) you have been ... !' (5b, 6) injected into the first question (5b), and added to the second question (v. 6), both noting in mocking tones that Edom has been dispossessed. It then concludes with a threefold statement of treachery by Edom's so-called allies (7a-c), ending with a charge of stupidity on Edom's part (7d).

5 '**If** thieves came to you, if plunderers (came) at night
   —**how** you have been destroyed!—
   would they not steal only what they wanted?
   If grape-gatherers came to you,
   would they not leave gleanings?
6 **How** Esau has been pillaged, his treasures searched out!'

7 'All your allies have deceived you, they have driven you to your borderlands; your confederates have prevailed against you; (those who ate) your bread have set a trap for you—
Nobody understands what has happened'.

The comparable Jeremiah text differs in clause order. Obadiah's question of how thieves operate is the second question in Jer. 49.9, the gleaning question being placed ahead of it. The two mocking statements prefaced by 'how!' are absent from Jeremiah 49, which also lacks the taunt that Edom's friends have worked against her. Also missing from Jeremiah 49 is the final note of contempt that Edomites have no understanding of what they have done, nor of what has been done to them. Edomite foolishness is then a theme taken up again in Obadiah, in the following section, vv. 8-10. In Jeremiah's case, the loss of wisdom and understanding is found earlier, in 49.7 as a prelude to the conditional questions rather than as a conclusion.

Exegesis

An immediate question relates to the nuance of the verbs used in these conditional statements. The Hebrew perfect that is used to refer to the thieves cites a possible but timeless scenario; the imperfect forms that are used in the apodosis following the question (Hebrew $h^a l\hat{o}$') are likewise timeless, 'would they not X?' (vv. 5b, c). These are not predictive statements. The clauses introduced by the exclamatory adverb 'eyk (vv. 5b, 6) clearly refer to a completed situation, thus a past state. The comment is expressing Judaean joy over what has happened to Edom subsequent to their participation in the attack on Jerusalem.

It should be noted that the two rhetorical questions in Obad. 5 about the thieves and gleaners have a different nuance from those in Jer. 49.9-11. The Jeremiah text implies that thieves and gleaners traditionally take only what they want or value, then depart, so there is always something remaining after they leave. This contrasts with the way in which God has dealt with Edom, namely by stripping it bare and leaving nothing behind, without friends or hiding place. For Obadiah, the questions imply that there was nothing left by either the thieves or the gleaners; all was taken by Edom's accomplices and 'friends', who stripped it and occupied its territory, pushing the Edomites to the very borders of their land. More to the point, Edomites do not comprehend how they have been tricked by those with whom they consorted.

While the illustration of thieves stealing from one's home is readily understandable, the case of grape-gatherers or gleaners is one based on the custom or law that harvesters of fruit, grain and vegetable crops intentionally leave behind a certain amount for the poor to glean (Lev. 19.9-10; Deut. 24.21); unlike the thief, gleaners must not strip the crop completely.

Verse 7 begins with an adverbial phrase stressing how the associates of Edom, 'your covenanted peoples', drove them to the very borders of their land. It is further stressed in v. 7b with a parallel phrase, literally 'peoples of your peace' having deceived Edom and prevailed against them. Edom may have thought itself on a par with the great powers, but in fact advantage was taken by those more powerful whom they thought were allies. Edom had been duped.

Verse 7c begins with an isolated phrase, 'for your bread', the text obviously missing something important. However, in the context of allies taking advantage of Edom, some parallel thought can be assumed, with the phrase itself possibly a metaphor for 'associates', those who shared food. It continues with 'they put a wound under you (or, in your place)'. Of course this seems to make little sense, but it is possible that the noun generally meaning 'wound' ($m\bar{a}z\hat{o}r$) is incorrectly written and should read $m\bar{a}\underline{s}\hat{o}r$, 'snare/trap'. That is what they have placed in Edom's way to take advantage of them. The point is that the former colleagues have taken advantage of Edom, but Edom has failed to realize what has happened. Hence the punchline in v. 7d—'you have no understanding of what has happened to you!' While the statement is vague, the context clearly infers Edom's ignorance, first in participating in the attack, and secondly in failing to see the result of that participation. Her allies, those in covenant with her, in the 587 adventure have tricked her and pushed her troops to the border regions, implying an occupation force.

Verses 8-10 Edom's Wisdom and Power Destroyed

8 'Was it not on that day', says the Lord, 'I destroyed the wise out of Edom, and understanding out of Mount Esau?'
9 'Your warriors were shattered, O Teman, such that everyone from Mount Esau was cut off'.
10 'For the slaughter and violence done to your brother Jacob, may shame cover you, and may you be cut off forever'.

The section begins with an unusual question, 'Was/Is it not in that day . . . says the Lord?' It introduces the section to give the impression that these words are divine speech and that the following first-person address outlines divine action. The question is whether it is referring to past or to future action. On the grounds that Obadiah is a prophetic text and that the initial verb, a perfect with prefixed *waw* (Heb *wᵉha'ᵃbadtî*), is serving as a future marker, many regard this section as promising future divine action against Edom. However, in light of vv. 5-6 and their description of past activity, and the keyword connection with v. 7 with its mocking of Edomite lack of wisdom—its lack of *tᵉbûnâ*, 'understanding', in v. 7d and v. 8b—this new section can justifiably be seen as expanding on the theme of its ignorance. Edom has failed to comprehend its new desperate situation because God destroyed its sages and denied it an understanding of what had happened to it. Jeremiah 49.7 also evidences these same sentiments, so it is clear that the community regarded Edom's alleged wisdom as folly; it did not prevent the nation making a foolish decision to join the battle for Jerusalem.

There seems to have been a view at the time that Edom was a source of wisdom. Perhaps that sense is evident in the book of Job, which may well have an Edomite setting, while the name Eliphaz, one of Job's counsellors, at least may have its roots there. If this be the case, then Judaean scoffing at wise Edom's folly is understandable.

The second matter of which Edom was so proud, its military might, was also decimated, with the result that vast numbers of the population were 'cut off', a verb used twice for emphasis in vv. 9-10. In describing the shattering of the Edomite infantry, the editor has given a reason for such happening, that is: 'so that they might be cut off from Mount Esau'. The proper noun Teman, the name of one of Esau's grandsons and thus of a tribe within Edom, was also that given to a geographical area in the central part of the region. As such, it is used here to represent the entire territory of Edom. It becomes clear that vv. 5-7 and vv. 8-9 are all about the past and what has happened. Set against the backdrop of the message in vv. 1b-4, the editor has outlined Edom's fate since participating in the 587 BCE attack on Jerusalem. Arrogant but ignorant Edom has been 'brought down'.

Verse 10 uses an imperfective verb as a jussive, a volitional call for action against Esau/Edom. Based on the tradition of their being 'brothers', the editor, on behalf of the descendants of Jacob, calls for divine action against Edom. Not only have they been 'cut off', the call now is for them to be 'cut off forever'. In this way the editor closes off the review of what Edom has done and suffered in preparation for the calls for divine action that follow the pivotal verse, v. 11.

Verse 11 The Core Charge against Edom

This verse is the numerically central verse, the pivot around which the document revolves; it states the basic charge Judaeans had against Edom—on the occasion of the attack on Jerusalem, '*you* were like one of them!' Any historical relationship between the two 'brothers' was now destroyed by Edom's treachery. While identifying the central verse in an individual book was a Masoretic device to allow checking by copyists to ensure that their copy was as accurate as possible, there was also a functional purpose in many cases, especially in the Minor Prophets; the central verse could mark a significant point of transition, as it does particularly well in Joel 2.17. In Obadiah, that transition at v. 11 was to a more vocal accusation levelled against Edom in a series of eight negative admonitions (vv. 12-14). The anger noted within those accusations is reflective of the anger expressed in Psalm 137.

11 On the day that you stood against (it), on the day that strangers captured his
  wealth, and foreigners entered his gates and cast lots for Jerusalem,
    you too were like one of them.

Functionally, the verse slowly builds tension, repeating 'on the day of your . . .' in its two opening clauses. Participles describe the Edomites 'standing against' Judah and foreigners stripping treasures in v. 11a, b. This is followed by two verbal clauses describing how strangers entered Jerusalem and cast lots for the plunder in v. 11c, d. The angry outburst is palpable as the final clause emphatically charges the Edomites—'*you* were (just) like one of them'. This is the role of the central verse in this collection.

Verse 11 begins with a reference to 'the day . . .', clearly referencing that past occasion when the Edomites stood with the enemy, not with the Judaeans. The Hebrew adverb *minneged,* 'over against', implies deliberate opposition. Edom was no different from the strangers and foreigners who ravaged Jerusalem; brotherly feelings were set aside as Edom joined the invaders in entering the city and stripping Jerusalem of its treasures—though Heb. *ḥēyl* has a broad application that could refer to power as well as material goods. The metaphor of casting lots for Jerusalem portrays Judah's enemies dividing up the spoils of victory. While the casting of lots has a definite religious significance as a means of determining the will of God, used metaphorically it can also carry a negative tone as is implied here (see also Joel 3.2-3).

Verses 12-14 Edom's Treachery Described

A series of eight negative imperatives gives vent to the anger Judaeans felt toward Edom. Each of the eight follows the fixed form: 'you should not have . . . on the day (occasion) of . . .' and relates to Edom's gloating, cheering over Judah's demise when attacking in 587 BCE. The section leads then into vv. 15-18, in which the Judaeans call for revenge on Edom for its participation in the attack on Jerusalem. The eight accusations are that Edom: (1) gloated; (2) rejoiced; (3) boasted (literally 'made your mouth big'); (4) invaded; (5) joined in; (6) looted; (7) intercepted those fleeing; (8) handed over survivors. The form then describes the 'Day' or occasion as one of distress, ruin and calamity for Judah.

12 But you should not have gloated over your brother
    on the day of his misfortune;
  you should not have rejoiced over the people of Judah
    on the day of their ruin;
  you should not have boasted
    on the day of distress.
13 You should not have entered the gate of my people
    on the day of their calamity;
  you should not have joined in the gloating over Judah's disaster
    on the day of his calamity;
  you should not have looted his goods
    on the day of his calamity.

14 You should not have stood at the crossings to cut off his fugitives;
   you should not have handed over his survivors
      on the day of distress.

The repetition of the form allows the reader to sense the level of anger felt by the Judaeans as they castigated the Edomites for their treachery. It also echoes the sentiments of Ps. 137.7, with its reference to the 'day' of Jerusalem's destruction in 587. The form uses a play on words as it was foreigners (Heb *nokrîm*) in v. 11 who brought such distress or calamity (Heb *nokrô*) upon Judah. Another play is the use of the noun *'ēyd*, 'calamity', three times in v. 13, for it sounds very like *'ᵉdôm*. The phonic closeness would not be missed by an audience.

The negative imperatives use *'al* as the negating particle to express a strong denunciation, differing from the form in the Ten Commandments where the simple *lô'*, 'not', is used. The verbs are jussive in form, but the syntax has been read in two ways: (1) as denouncing a past act—'you should not have gloated' (as NRSV); and (2) as indicating a past situation that continues into the present and beyond—'Do not (continue to) gloat'. The reference obviously is back to the event itself, but whether it has in mind that past act only or Edom's ongoing and presently held views has to be determined by the wider content. When one considers the full content of vv. 12-14 and the references to looting, to preventing anyone escaping from Jerusalem, or handing over survivors, these are clearly not current activities, so a rendering that reflects past behaviour is to be preferred.

The verbal attack on Edom in these verses is founded on the notion that there was a traditional familial relationship between Judaeans and Edomites. Edomite willingness and eagerness to join Judah's enemies to inflict this humiliation on Judah (v. 12) made the Edomite treachery all the more painful for Judah. A mocking tone is very evident in this verse as tiny Edom (v. 2) is said to have a big mouth—the Hebrew is literally 'you should not have enlarged your mouth'—as it sought to be at one with the 'big boys' attacking Judah.

Throughout this section the use of third-person reference to Judah suggests that the editor is at some distance removed from the event and is clearly reporting rather than voicing his personal feelings. However, v. 13 focused on the act of invasion itself and the looting of the city, under the metaphor of entering 'the gates of *my* people'. This is one of the few places in the text where a first-person pronoun is used, perhaps to imply God as the speaker, though that is not the necessary conclusion to be drawn. 'My people' can simply be the speaker identifying with fellow Judaeans. The trifold repetition of *'ēyd* as 'calamity' at the end of each line emphasizes the distress and anger felt toward Edom and its past actions.

Verse 14 emphasized the Edomite treatment of those who sought to flee the conflict but found themselves captured and handed over to be exiled. It presumably has a historical basis in that it appears to recall the story of Zedekiah and his party's attempt to flee the Babylonians and escape entrapment in the city (see 2 Kgs 25.4-6). It accuses the Edomites of preventing their escape via the Jordan river crossing point to the Arabah. The Hebrew noun from the root *plṭ* refers to those who have escaped from or survived a crisis, elsewhere called a 'remnant'. (See below v. 17.)

Verses 15-18 Edomite Treachery to Be Repaid.

This section calls for punishment upon the nations and Edom and expresses hope that Judaeans will be compensated for what was lost. It begins with the announcement that the Day of the Lord has come near; it is very present. The verbs throughout are jussives rather than prophetic perfects as the Judaeans call for the nations, and then especially Edom, to suffer as they had made Judah suffer. Its sentiments are similar to those expressed in Ps. 137.7-9. So:

15 Truly, the day of the Lord is imminent against all the nations.
   As you have done, so let it be done to you; may your deeds return on your own head.
16 Indeed, as you have drunk on my holy mountain, may all the nations around you drink;
   drink and gulp down, and may they be as though they had never been.
17 But on Mount Zion let there be those who escape, and let it be holy;
   And may the house of Jacob take possession of those who dispossessed them.
18 May the house of Jacob be a fire, the house of Joseph a flame, and the house of Esau stubble;
   to burn and consume them,
   and let there be no survivor of the house of Esau;
   the Lord has indeed spoken.

The section is introduced by the Hebrew particle *kî*, here with the emphatic sense of 'indeed/truly' rather than 'for', as it does not explain or give the results of the previous accusations in vv. 12-14. Rather, it introduces a new direction, turning from the past to something immediate.

Following the announcement in v. 15a two clauses follow, vv. 15b-16, each applying the principle for just punishment, namely 'an eye for an eye', and demanding that justice be done. Each begins with the same Hebrew phrase *ka'ᵃšer*, which signals two comparative clauses—here, 'just as (you did/drank)' with the revenge action using the same verbs—'may it be done/may they drink...' These are followed in vv. 17-18 by calls for a reversal, for Judah to be rescued, to regain what was lost, and to bring a complete end to Edom. It concludes with the form 'says the Lord', underlined by the emphatic particle *kî*, as found at the beginning of the section.

This reading regards the section as a discrete unit, with v. 15a and v. 18d bracketing the calls with traditional prophetic forms provided by the editor. These verbless forms are designed to give a 'prophetic' cast to the section, which is really a plea for urgent divine action on Judah's behalf.

Verse 15. The Day of the Lord, that time when God is believed to act on some future occasion, is described by the Hebrew adverb as *qārôb*, 'near'. Its nearness can serve both temporal and locational descriptions as well as intimate relationships. The closeness, be it temporal or locational, is here imminent, not some vague and uncertain future. Although the audience appears to be the foreign nations, including Edom, they have no ears to hear, for these are words directed at the Judaean audience, as are all calls against foreigners. These words are expressive of the people's joy at the imminent revenge that they wish to see brought upon Edom. The remainder of the unit then continues with the jussive verbs that call God to act now.

Verses 15b-16 echo sentiments expressed in Ps. 137.8. Whatever the enemies had done to Judah is what Judah wishes to see fall on them. The Hebrew verb *šûb*, 'turn/return', speaks of actions taken coming back to bite those who advanced them (see also Joel 3.4, 7 etc.). In v. 15b the principle is enunciated in general terms—it has become a trope—and in v. 16 the principle is exemplified using the metaphor of drinking. Although Edom is not specified in this section, it has to be assumed that Edom is its main focus—the 'you' in v. 15b is singular as it is in the central verse—with all the participating nations as the agents carrying out God's punishment. On the other hand, in v. 16 'you' is plural, so there is a slight issue with consistency, implying that the nations are also embraced within Judah's request for divine action, unless suddenly the editor has used the plural to refer to Edom alone. If that is the case, then the following 'they' refers to the nations as those who will 'drink' up Edom. The section pleads with God to punish Edom, extending the drinking metaphor to emphasize that they should not just 'drink' but 'drink and gulp down' Edom. Unfortunately, the second Hebrew verb involved here is rare and thus of slightly uncertain meaning. Some link it with drinking the 'cup of judgment', but the general context suggests that it refers to drinking to excess since it is a metaphor for annihilation. The first-person reference to '*my* holy mountain' may be a deliberate choice to imply that God is the speaker.

The biblical principle of an eye for an eye, that any punishment should fit the crime (Deut. 19.21), does not apply here as Judah cries out that more severe punishment be given to Edom than Edom inflicted upon Judah. God's holy mountain had been desecrated, so the call is for the enemy to be so reduced 'as though they had never been'. Judah wants their complete destruction. The hyperbole in this plea is on the same level as that of Ps. 137.9.

In v. 17 the initial *waw* connector is the adversative 'but', contrasting the punishment of the enemies with the great future asked for Judah. The tone changes from one of anger at what Edom had done to one of joy at what Judah expects to see happen to its enemy. The plea is that Mount Zion will once again be sanctified, its desecration reversed, that Mount Zion will be a place of escape or sanctuary. The literal phrase 'let it be an escape' uses a nominal form of *plṭ*, which mostly refers to people who have escaped, a remnant or portion of a larger number (see above v. 14 and Joel 3.5 [Heb.]). It was a general term with wide application rather than referring to one specific group. The phrase here in Obad. 17a is found also in Joel 2.32, hinting at its general and wide use during the period to describe any cohort who managed to escape a crisis.

Continuing the theme of reversal or revenge, the plea is that the 'house of Jacob', the people of Judah, Edom's erstwhile brother, take possession of those who dispossessed them. More precisely, it calls for Judah's troops to occupy Edom. This call to 'possess' Edom introduces the verb (Heb. *yāraš*) that will appear three times in vv. 19-20 to summarize the broader activity noted.

Verse 18 changed the metaphor within the request to that of fire and its impact. The 'house of Jacob', or parallel 'house of Joseph' representing the 'pure' lineage of the present peoples, is likened to a fire that burns the stubble in the fields after harvest. The stubble is Edom, a remnant of a different kind! May they be burned so totally that there will be no survivor from this conflagration. Throughout this verse the imagery of a 'house' is chosen as a keyword to represent the family or entire tribe whether of Judah or the Edomites. Here in vv. 17-18 those who escape are the ones who call for possessing Edom, burning and consuming its people.

The section is then brought to a conclusion with an editorial addition: 'for(?) the Lord has spoken' to mark its independence. There is an identical form in Joel 3.8 that uses a strong (piel) form of the verb 'speak' and in a similar context to that found here in Obadiah. This insertion by the editor appears to authenticate the preceding material, but the particle *kî* at this point may be better read as the emphatic 'truly/indeed' as in v. 15. If this be

Exegesis 25

the case, then the editor has used it to bracket the pleas that are the feature of vv. 15-18.

Verses 19-21 Edom Dispossessed

From a more poetic style in vv. 15-18 this section moves to narrative format built around a key verb *yāraš*, 'possess', which calls for Edom and other surrounding enemy territories to be occupied once again by Judah. The key verb is prominent in Deuteronomy's descriptions of the land being given to the Israelites as their 'possession' (e.g. Deut. 5.31, 33 etc.).

19 So let those of the Negeb possess Mount Esau, and those of the Shephelah the land of the Philistines;
   May they possess the land of Ephraim and the land of Samaria, and Benjamin possess Gilead.
20 And let the exiles of the ramparts of the Israelites possess the Canaanites as far as Zarephath;
   and the exiles of Jerusalem who are in Sepharad possess the towns of the Negeb.
21 And let those who have been rescued go up to Mount Zion to rule Mount Esau;
   and let the kingdom be the Lord's.

The Hebrew text in this section is somewhat cryptic on first reading, the challenge coming from the use of geographical regions, such as the Negeb and Shephelah, to represent the Judaeans or peoples living within them. Presumably this accounts for the use of the third-person plural form in the opening verb (*yārᵉšû*). Issues in the Hebrew text need to be taken up, but initially one can acknowledge that the overall sense is of Edom being dispossessed and the old southern kingdom of Judah restored in expanded dimensions. Many scholars read these texts as prophetic, detailing promises of a new future; this reader retains the view that the text is another version of the plea for Edom to be dealt with in the same manner as it treated Jerusalem and its people.

Reading the verbs as jussives, as pleas for divine action, the point being made is that Judaeans who have been exiled to the regions bordering Judah, call on God to re-establish God's kingdom. It calls for a move against those occupying land traditionally believed to have been assigned to the Israelites, from the Negeb in the south to Samaria and beyond in the north and extending into the lowlands to the west now occupied by the Philistines. This would be a plea for the restoration of the land as promised to Israel, and as allegedly so held in the time of the great kings, David and Solomon.

Although Edom, according to Deuteronomy, was given to the Edomites to possess as descendants of Esau (e.g. Deut. 2.5), now Judah pleads for Edom's territory to become part of an even wider 'kingdom of God'. Current inhabitants of the traditional land and those returning exiles, spoken of as 'the rescued ones', are to rule Edom from Mount Zion (v. 21). The vision calls for the restitution of the land as promised.

Verse 19a opens with the Hebrew verb $w^ey\bar{a}r^e\check{s}\hat{u}$ ('Now may they possess' or 'So, let them possess') of which the subject 'they' is believed to refer to the peoples of the Negeb and the peoples of the Shephelah. In other words, the verb has two subjects, and the areas or peoples that they are expecting to take over are identified respectively as 'Mount Esau' and 'the Philistines'. As noted, place or regional names are substituting for those who live there. The Negeb as a regional name is the largely desert area south of Judah, with Beersheba at its northern border. It was an area into which Edomite peoples from the mountains to the east had moved following the events of 587 BCE (Ezek. 36.5). In this section the regional name Negeb serves also as a rhetorical feature, as an inclusion that brackets vv. 19-20.

The second half of v. 19a reads '. . . and the Shephelah . . .' This is the region between the central mountains and the Mediterranean coast, so the slopes and lower lands to the west of Jerusalem–Hebron spine. It was and remains a more fertile and well-watered region. It was into this region's southern areas that the Philistines or Sea Peoples had moved some centuries before, after they had established a foothold on the southwestern or Mediterranean coast of Judah. The call in the text is for both the Judaeans in the Negeb to occupy Mount Esau, that is, Edom, and those living in the Shephelah or lowlands to occupy the Philistine territory to the west.

Verse 19b repeats the verb $y\bar{a}r^e\check{s}\hat{u}$, but no subject is specified, so one has to assume that the subject remains the Judaeans in the two regions who are urged to take back Ephraim, the former northern kingdom and its capital Samaria. The reference to 'fields' in these two latter regions may reflect their more pastoral or agricultural context.

The final clause is literally '. . . and Benjamin, the Gilead'. The previous verbs obviously are meant to serve this phrase as well. Benjamin's tribal area was formerly to the north of Judah and incorporated into the kingdom of Judah; it is called upon to occupy the region of Gilead. In the division of the land reported in Numbers 32, Gilead was assigned to Reuben, Gad and half of Manasseh. It was a fertile and well-watered hilly region to the northwest of what was called Transjordan, with a border that extended as far north as the Jabbok river. The call here is for the Benjaminites to cross the Jordan river and occupy the region of Gilead as those tribes once had done.

Verse 20a, b reveals two parallel pleas for the people exiled (*gālut*) as a result of the deportations of 587 BCE. The Hebrew text is obviously problematic: the first plea seemingly relates to 'those exiled of this rampart (Heb. *ḥēl*)', something that NRSV renders as 'those who are in Halah', while others suggest it refers to an army. The Hebrew noun can also mean 'strength', a more abstract notion. The noun, if understood to mean 'ramparts', implies a location of some kind, but one that is unclear unless v. 20b is viewed as parallel, in which case the ramparts may well be those of Jerusalem. Adding to the challenge is that it then continues as literally: '. . . for the Israelites who [are] Canaanites as far as Zarephath', where 'Canaanites' seemingly refers to Canaanite territory that northern Israel is to possess. Clearly, the Hebrew text is corrupt, and this is reflected in the various translations available, all of which have made guesses as to possible meanings. The LXX rendering is of little assistance in clarifying the text. The mention of Zarephath points to a location just south of Sidon on the coast and an erstwhile northern boundary to the Canaanite territory. Presumably this is a reference to exiles from the northern kingdom returning to regain their land, but there is no certainty.

Parallel to the first reference to exiled people is the call for those *gālut*, exiled, of Jerusalem now in Sepharad to regain the towns in the Negeb. Sepharad's location, if it is real, is unknown, despite numerous possibilities having been suggested, including the Greek islands, Sardis in Asia Minor and one ancient translation, Syriac, rendering it as Spain. That these exiles might return and occupy the southern desert fringe, the Negeb, seems an unlikely locale for them. Regardless of Sepharad's precise location, what the call does envisage is a reinvigorated kingdom inhabited by Judah's returned exiles in an expanded territory incorporating the fullest extent of the earlier idealized unified kingdom of Israel.

The final verse, v. 21, consists of two calls: first, to 'those who have been rescued' (reading the Hebrew as emended to *mushā'îm*) and those living on Mount Zion. They are urged to go occupy and rule over (*šāpaṭ*) Mount Esau. In other words, once the Judaean exiles have returned from the places to which they had been taken, the call is for them to rise up and take over the Edomite territory and its people. The second and final call is for the kingdom once more to be seen as belonging to YHWH (v. 21c). The words are full of hope and anticipation for a revitalized kingdom of God.

In reality, the 'remnant' (*pᵉleyṭâ*) in v. 17 and the 'saved' in v. 21 probably refer to much the same cohort of people, for not all those who had been taken into exile took advantage of the opportunity to return to Jerusalem and Judah when it was given by the Persians in 538 BCE. Many had established themselves in their new environment, and many of those born into that world had adapted, such that Babylon and other parts of the region to which they had been exiled had become 'home'. They saw no need to return to an unfamiliar Judaea.

Postscript

Reading Obadiah as a carefully edited and structured document raises questions about its prophetic qualifications. While its incorporation within the Scroll of the Twelve suggests that it is 'prophetic', it is now clear that Obadiah does not fit within a traditional definition; rather, it is a collation of oral materials known and repeated throughout the post-587 BCE Israelite community, expressing its anger, calling for revenge against those who destroyed Jerusalem and exiled its people. The material had close connections with the prophetic community but was not confined there. While aimed widely against the nations, it targeted Edom in particular.

Obadiah and Deuteronomy

The Deuteronomic vision of a land given by God to his people Israel (Deut. 1.8, 21) underlies the longings expressed in this document. This was much more than a simple case of long-term habitation of a space; it was the fact that Israel believed the land was ceded to them by divine promise, and a promise that they saw reaching back to the ancestor Abraham. Being attacked and driven out of that land by enemies that included a supposed 'relative' was a major trauma; it called into question their identity, their sense of place, and the power of the God who had made such a promise.

With a firm belief that their God Yahweh was the one who held sway over all nations, appealing to God to deal with those nations that threatened Judah's very existence was a theme built into the people's minds and hopes. Lament liturgies and psalmic expression, both individual and corporate, gave vent to their frustrations when events overtook them. Although most of the lament psalms expressed innocence, believing much suffering caused by 'enemies' of all kinds was unearned and undeserved, calls for God to intervene on the people's behalf were a major component of religious life. Obadiah evidences something of the depth of feeling, the emotion, attached to cries for divine intervention and for divine justice to be meted out upon those who had not just desecrated a sacred space, Jerusalem, but who demonstrated thereby a total disregard for Israel's God.

Obadiah and Psalm 137

In calling for God to act against these enemies, Obadiah's report offers another example of the way people responded to the trauma of 587 BCE; it gathers together a number of the established tropes that had developed over the years since.

The vehemence of the longing expressed in Psalm 137 with regard to events surrounding the sack of Jerusalem exhibits itself here in Obadiah. It demonstrates another facet of the human difficulty of reconciling the notion of a just and loving God with devastating events that overtake one. Despite the fact that ancient prophets and the Deuteronomic theologians had tried to explain the demise of Judah as a well-deserved divine punishment, anger, resentment, and a longing for revenge were poured out as 'normal' human reactions to the resultant suffering. Many readers are troubled by this desire for revenge, for long-held resentment, believing that it is inconsistent with a biblically rooted religious faith. However, it remains as a reality that each person of faith must confront and deal with in a manner that makes a religious commitment something of value.

Reading Obadiah as a prophetic assurance of a beneficial outcome to the Judaean call for revenge does not assist most readers who struggle with the profound issue of what it is to be human in an enigmatic world.

Fulfilment?

Reading the text as prophetic in the promissory sense has to acknowledge that the hyperbole used to express those promises results in the challenge that such promises as are listed in vv. 19-21 are/were not possible of literal fulfilment. While some wish to project what they regard as the physical and political promises of Obadiah into a spiritual dimension, seeking to establish links to the New Testament and the church, others see the promises realized in the establishment of today's State of Israel, a political entity that has a tentative foothold in the region. Neither of these readings is consistent with what Obadiah 'promised'; neither can be sustained as a reflection of what Obadiah longed to see without acknowledging the preconceptions from which such reading is done. While no reading can be free of preconceptions, one must honour the text in its context and seek to minimize all more obvious eisegetical readings.

A Conclusion

This reading began with a question about the nature of the Obadiah document. This reader has concluded that what is titled 'Obadiah's Vision' is the final editor's collected and edited report drawing on some of the expressions of pain and resentment that circulated orally among Judaeans from the fall of Jerusalem in 587 BCE through the many ensuing years. Psalm 137 points to the possibility that many of the sayings were preserved within liturgical settings invoking divine aid. These expressions served as means to pour out anger and frustration at both the individual and collective level for what had happened to Judah and its people; it called upon God to avenge the sack of his dwelling place, to bring people back and to restore the kingdom to its original dimensions in the land as promised. While primarily aimed at vengeance upon Edom, it also swept up the nations in its call for divine punishment and the return of those Judaeans who had been led off into captivity.

Brief Bibliography

Allen, L.C., *The Books of Joel, Obadiah, Jonah and Micah* (NICOT; Grand Rapids, MI: Eerdmans, 1976).

Clark, D.G., N. Mundhenk, E. Nida and B. Price, *A Handbook on Obadiah* (New York: United Bible Societies, 1978–93).

Jepsen, A., '*chazah*', in G.J. Botterweck and H. Ringgren (eds.), *TDOT*, IV, pp. 280-90.

Mason, R., *Micah, Nahum and Obadiah* (T. & T. Clark Study Guides; Sheffield: Sheffield Academic Press, 1991).

Seitz, C.R., *The Goodly Fellowship of the Prophets* (Grand Rapids, MI; Baker Academic, 2009).

Stuart, D., *Hosea–Jonah* (WBC, 31; Dallas, TX: Word Books, 1987).

Thompson, J.A., *The Book of Obadiah* (Interpreter's Bible, 6; New York: Abingdon Press, 1956).

HAGGAI

A Commentary

Introduction

From Little Things Big Things Grow

The second shortest 'book' incorporated into the Old Testament is the 38-verse document named after the prophet Haggai; it is hardly worthy to be considered a 'book' as it covers little more than a printed page in modern Bibles. Despite its brevity, it throws a spotlight on the role of the prophet in ensuring that the Temple was resurrected from its ruins to play its role in postexilic Judaism's religious life. What we have in Haggai is a brief narrative report by an unnamed editor as to Haggai's mission to have the Temple rebuilt and functioning. How a document so short, and a prophetic word so limited, played vital roles in the life of the Jewish community in Jerusalem in 520 BCE is what the commentary will explore.

In 538 BCE following the Persian victory over Babylonia the previous year, Cyrus the Great signed a document permitting the Judaeans, who had been living in exile for some 50 years, the opportunity to return to Jerusalem to rebuild their lives. This included rebuilding the Temple that Nebuchadnezzar and his troops had destroyed in 587 BCE. Ezra 1.2-4 reports a version of the Cyrus edict reflecting the Persian leader's more open and generous attitude to the many peoples who had been taken into exile by the Babylonians. As for the Judaeans, not only were they given permission to return, much of the booty stolen by the Babylonians was returned to them, including gold and silver objects taken from the Temple. Ezra also records neighbours of the departing Jews offering them gold and silver vessels along with 'animals and valuable gifts' (Ezra 1.6). Ezra 2 lists the names of a number of those who chose to return, but it is obvious that many chose not to take the opportunity, having settled into life in the general region from which their ancestor Abraham was said to have emigrated more than a millennium before.

Cyrus remained on the Persian throne until 530 BCE and was succeeded by his son Cambyses, but he died in July 522 BCE. The throne was then taken by Darius I, who continued the Persian policy established by Cyrus. He appointed Zerubbabel as the new 'governor' of the province of Judaea. It was in Darius's second year in charge that Haggai the prophet is said to have received a divine call, though one can wonder whether he may well have had a prophetic prehistory of which we are told nothing.

On Reading Haggai

Reading Haggai can be compared to reading someone else's mail. In Haggai, one is reading a third-person report of messages passing between a prophet, Haggai, and his community, none of whom are known to the reader, who represent a cultural and religious world historically removed by two millennia from one's own, a report read in translation from an ancient foreign language; it is a reading fraught with issues for the keenest reader to consider.

When working from one language and culture to another, similarity rather than equivalence is the communication goal, for there is no complete overlap or identity between any two languages, even between dialects of the same language. The concepts and jargon, the nuances that resonate immediately with native speakers of a language, are such that non-native speakers and readers almost certainly do not notice them. As a result, many cultural elements lying within a communication remain unseen and unheard by the translator, not fully understood or misinterpreted. Added to these is the issue of certain words in the source language having a broad semantic range from which the translator can choose only one of many possible renderings for inclusion in its text. These facts make the task of translating and interpreting a document like Haggai a huge challenge, but they also offer a great reward to those who would take up the task, aware of the issues involved.

Haggai, a report provided to a tiny tribal audience in the ancient enclave of Judaea but now available to a global community for which it was never intended, belongs to a specific context. How does one in the twenty-first century understand that report, and does its message have any possible relevance for readers today? These and related questions are what a modern commentary on Haggai must consider, and then hope to minimize any alien values, personal limitations and presuppositions of numerous kinds—linguistic, cultural, religious—that one might import, even unconsciously, while seeking to uncover the specific ideas in and behind that text. Once having identifed them, each can be considered for its potential importance.

The point about 'minimizing alien values' is an important one. When reading a document intended for some other audience than that of the modern reader, a document that is the product of and that addresses social, political and ideological circumstances so distant from the present, there is the constant 'danger' of reading into the text one's own notions and personal biases and of adding interpretations that do not belong. When this happens, the value of any conclusion drawn is questionable.

While Haggai was included in the sacred writings of the pre-Christian Jewish communities, it was taken over into the emerging Christian world as part of its own sacred Scriptures, with the inevitable result that Haggai was, and continues to be, read by that community from within the perspective, or perspectives, of the diversified Christian world. This is one example of a reading method that adopts the so-called canonical approach, that is, reading Haggai as part of the church's wider canon, that sees the New Testament as the goal of a whole-of-Bible trajectory from Genesis to Revelation. A christological reading that sees Jesus as the fulfilment of all that was promised in the Old Testament, as for example in Matthew's Gospel, is acceptable only if one first acknowledges that it involves imposing a later theological design on the ancient text, one that could not have been intended by the original editor's report. No modern reader of Haggai is immune from the potential 'danger' of misunderstanding, or even distorting, what the sixth-century BCE Judaean community may have heard and understood of Haggai's intent.

The present author believes that it is possible to identify, describe and evaluate a number of Haggai's basic notions and concerns about God and community, that is, his theology, but makes no claim to have escaped the trap of reading alien values and ideology into the text of Haggai. The following commentary is offered as another possible reading that seeks to honour the original text and context, while remaining cognizant of the challenges in doing so.

A Reading Plan
There are four particular elements operative in my reading of Haggai:

A. I have given considerable weight to the oral nature of prophetic presentations and to the complex transmission and editing processes that have culminated in Haggai as a written document. I have read these 38 verses with an eye to this process insofar as I understand the nature of oral 'literature'. I understand that it is the final editor who has shaped this report, drawing upon the living stories and oral traditions about Haggai circulating at the time. Whether he knew Haggai closely or was a supporter of the role Haggai played in 520 BCE Judaea is unclear, but he has reported what he heard and knew, seemingly fully sympathetic with the prophet's viewpoint; the editor shared his knowledge of the prophet with his Jerusalem audience, incorporating a report of communal responses to that message. I use 'editor' throughout, aware that 'he' is representative of all those who contributed to the preservation and shaping of the text as we now have it.

B. I assume that the prophet presented his oral messages on a variety of occasions, in numerous settings, and over what is said to have been at least a three-month period. The date on which Haggai is said to have received a message is little more than a marker provided by the redactor for structural purposes, for the real challenges to do with the Temple rebuilding would need to have been put to the whole community frequently throughout the building process. What I call a 'flat' or unimaginative reading of Haggai treats the text as reporting a one-time announcement following initial receipt of the message, something like 'Message One received: Message One delivered', a view that fails to consider the very nature of living oral transmission and memory. I assume that Haggai spoke to the leaders regularly, separately as well as together, given the different responsibilities each held.

C. Having spent almost all my career in various cultures and communities in East Asia, I am deeply conscious of how sustained 'foreign' experience may and does reshape one's early notion of self and the belief system inherited from one's family. For those living in a cultural world different from that of the previous generation of one's family, whether as expatriate workers, immigrants or refugees, the experience of straddling two cultures impacts on the perception of both. Consequently, I have wondered about the possible impact of a lengthy Babylonian exile on those Jews like Haggai, Zerubbabel and Joshua, whom I assume were born in Babylonia, born to Jewish parents yet raised in that alien environment, growing up with Aramaic as their new *lingua franca* but now returning to an unfamiliar and devastated Jerusalem. It has raised for me a number of questions: What religious identity did each have? Their shared language was no longer the Hebrew of the ancient Scriptures, nor were they familiar with Temple ritual. Certainly, many had kept alive their old traditions in their homes in exile via its major festivals; but how deep were these cultural roots, for many of this second generation, refugees from the only world they had known, Babylon, now seeking a new life in an unfamiliar 'home' land? I have tried to ponder what their priorities, hopes and goals might have been. More generally, it is true that for some, the experience of living between two cultures can be traumatic, leading one to resist the new, the different, such that one's earlier inherited or first-culture views become more firmly held and valued. This is something that I see in Haggai's embrace of the comforting nationalistic ideology of Deuteronomy, or as upheld in the story of Daniel (Dan. 1.8-17). In other folk, an openness to 'the other' creates a tension between the older family traditions and those of the new environment, such that one lives in the in-between 'third culture' that reshapes any latent ideas. This latter I see arguably present in Zerubbabel and Joshua; I assume that as both grew to adulthood in Babylonia they were heavily influenced by that world, its ideas and culture, resulting in an enlarged worldview, one that opened the door to their being offered leadership roles by the Persians. (See below 'On Haggai, Zerubbabel and Joshua'.)

D. I also admit to reading Haggai as 'witness' or 'testimony', that is, as a report of one man's witness to his beliefs and ideals, expressed in terms of a particular ideology or theology. Haggai the document is the reported witness of Haggai as one member of a cohort in the larger community, one within which there were multiple ideas about God, about life, and about selfhood, as is true of any human association. Haggai's point of view, determined by his Deuteronomic perspective on life (see below), has to be considered in the context of other views circulating at the time, for example, that of the sages. The worldview and perspective of these latter differ fundamentally from that of Haggai, for they were founded on broad human experience rather than dependent on an external source, a divine revelation to a small family tribe; the sages' views and advice were grounded in life experiences and reflection, shared with or held in common with international and intercultural bodies. Both perspectives, that of the prophet and that of the sage, are of value; and although it is obvious that the Jewish sages disagreed with many aspects of the other's perspective, nevertheless, both shared a common Jewish heritage, seeing themselves as members of a 'people of God' under covenant with Yahweh.

The reading strategy I have adopted means that one does not simply take the witness reported of Haggai as absolute, or read it unimaginatively (what I call a 'flat' reading), but read it as a report of the prophet's personal view dependent on a specific theological tradition, that of Deuteronomy. As such, it leads a reader to questions about the extent to which one's own experience of God or of 'the divine' accords with that of the witness being offered by Haggai. It is in dialogue with Haggai that one finds affirmation of, or further questions for, one's own ideology.

Haggai and Israel's Prophetic Tradition

The Hebrew Bible consists of three major divisions: Law (*tôrâ/torah*), Prophets (*nᵉbî'îm*), and Writings (*kᵉtûbîm*), or *Tanak* for short. The Prophets are further divided into Former and Latter Prophets. The Former Prophets, Joshua–2 Kings, highlight the exploits of prophets such as Deborah, Elijah, Elisha, and Nathan in the developing story of early Israel in the promised land. The Latter Prophets are written reports of the speeches attributed to Isaiah (and his cohort), Jeremiah, Ezekiel and 'the Twelve', the so-called Minor Prophets, 'minor' because the books that deal with their ministries are relatively short. The 'book' that bears the name of the prophet Haggai is the tenth in what has become the composite Scroll of the Twelve, the books listed from Hosea to Malachi. Haggai, as one of the Twelve, consists of a mere 38 verses, hardly qualifying to be called a book; it is more like a leaflet, a brief one-page document revealing, through the work of its editor, the particular concerns and advice of one of ancient Israel's least-known prophets. The Scroll of the Twelve is of a length not quite that of the Isaiah scroll discovered at Qumran, which is 734 cm. long. This makes Haggai's few words—surely it was not all Haggai spoke about over time—that are preserved in the Scroll of the Twelve even more significant, in the sense that its 38 verses must have been seen to have special merit for them to be included along with the more extensive records of prophets such as Hosea and Amos.

The Scroll of the Twelve contains a collection of prophetic speeches from the eighth century BCE attributed to Hosea and Amos; it includes a postexilic Joel, the story of Jonah, and concludes with the thoughts of Malachi, dating from sometime around 500–450 BCE. Thus, the Scroll of the Twelve, similar to the collection attached to Isaiah, gathers material that spans two centuries of collecting, editing and arranging. This was done by many hands who shaped the messages to address contemporary situations over that lengthy period, couching them within established literary forms. There is a clear historical order in the placement of the books of the Scroll of the Twelve that can account for Haggai being where it is in the list. The precise dating in 520 BCE locates Haggai along with his contemporary Zechariah but after Zephaniah, because both Haggai and Zechariah are clearly contemporaneous, perhaps the first postexilic prophets whose messages were considered worth retaining and reporting.

Several of the individual books now in the Scroll of the Twelve have been updated as part of their transmission history, as can be seen in the Judahite additions in Hosea (6.4-11) and Amos (9.11-15), prophets whose mission was essentially directed to the northern kingdom of Israel, and adding to their relevance to later generations and audiences in Judaea. In addition, there is evidence that in the gathering of the various books, further editorial work linked one book literarily with the one that follows in the list—e.g. Amos 1.2 repeats Joel 3.16; Nah. 1.3 repeats Mic. 7.18. In the case of Haggai, one could argue that Zeph. 3.14-20 anticipates a return to Jerusalem that is realized in Haggai. Perhaps this is a major reason for including and placing Haggai ahead of Zechariah 1–8, though they were both witnesses of those early postexilic times.

Haggai in Historical Context

Haggai, the document, consists of four dated elements: 1.1-15a; 1.15b–2.9; 2.10-19; 2.20-23. Each deals with issues that arose in Judaea during the early reign of the Persian King Darius I (522–486 BCE) following the death of his brother Cambyses and the release of the Judaean captives in Babylon by Cyrus in 538 BCE. Darius was met with revolts when first coming to power in 522 BCE, and as a result there is some question as to whether his first regnal year is to be counted from when that situation was resolved and there was greater stability in the empire, namely 521 BCE, or a year later in 520 BCE. There is a general consensus that 522 BCE can be affirmed as the beginning of his reign. Darius's administration began by dividing the empire into 30 satrapies with smaller divisions called provinces, of which Judaea was one.

The dates given to the four elements in Haggai locate the prophet in the second year of Darius's reign, in 520 BCE, to the specific day if not the hour, meaning that Haggai's recorded mission took place in the early postexilic period, a few years after a number of exiles had returned from Babylon to Jerusalem. By the time Haggai was active in his prophetic role in Jerusalem, Darius's situation had stabilized, and it was important for the Persians to have a compliant and 'friendly' provincial leader in Zerubbabel to provide a buffer against any potential Egyptian challenges. Additionally, Judaea was fortunate in that the Babylonians, unlike the Assyrians, had not flooded Judaea with captives from other parts of its empire, so Judaea remained a basically monocultural Jewish community.

Those exiles who chose to return to Judaea when offered the opportunity consisted essentially of people born in Babylonia during the 50 years of exile, 587–538 BCE. It seems unlikely that many, if any, of the cohort originally taken into custody in Babylon were still alive in 520 BCE, when Haggai's calling is said to have occurred. While the Jerusalem leadership and many of the elite were exiled in 587 BCE, it is estimated that the total number was somewhere between a few thousand and up to a maximum of twenty thousand. Actual numbers are difficult to ascertain, but Judah was not stripped of its population despite the material destruction of so much in and around the area of Jerusalem, the Temple suffering major damage and its treasures looted. Archaeological investigation shows that especially north of Jerusalem, around Mizpah, and south toward Bethlehem, life post-587 carried on throughout the period largely untroubled. It is important not to focus all attention on Jerusalem and the Temple because the bulk of the population post-538 was scattered throughout the entire region of the old kingdom of Judah. Archaeological research indicates that the area of old Jerusalem that was occupied after the exile was much smaller than that occupied prior to the exile, and its population also was smaller than in 587 BCE.

After 50 years of being in exile, many Jews chose to remain in Babylonia, having adapted to life there, so we can assume that those who returned from Babylon were primarily those who were determined to recover a more traditional and strict Jewish identity rather than adapt to foreign ways. Nostalgia for their old home and a continuing sense of their old identity meant that they had never given up hope of eventually returning to Judaea.

Following Cyrus's edict allowing the return, Judaea became a province of the Persian Empire, under its effective control and influence, with the administration in the hands of a 'governor', Sheshbazzar (538), and later Zerubbabel (520), while primary control was exercised through the Samaritans. The region was a sensitive one for the Persians as it was strategic, located on the border with Egypt, a potential rival to Persian power in the region. Having a compliant community in that location was to Persia's advantage. Jerusalem was now without king and Temple and had lost much of its former mystique and glory, but Zerubbabel's possible link with the Davidic dynasty and Haggai's promise in 2.20-23 may hint at hopes of a royal revival among the residents of Jerusalem.

Once arrived in Jerusalem, the domestic situation facing Haggai and his contemporaries was dire: difficult climatic conditions throughout the region, poor harvests of all kinds, and devastated towns and villages, combined with general despair at the onerous reconstruction task ahead of them, put the returnees under enormous pressure. Added to this there were doubts about Yahweh's covenant commitment, and all faced another round of national challenge, this time from an advanced Persian culture and its religious ideas. Another source of difficulty was opposition from the north by the so-called people of the land, a mixed community of peoples, Samaritans for the main part. They objected to any plans for rebuilding in Jerusalem, whether of the city walls or the Temple itself. It was Haggai's challenge to rouse the Judaeans, get the Temple rebuilding programme operative, and see it completed despite these hardships. That was not achieved until 516 BCE, some four years after Haggai began to exhort the people to make it their priority. Presumably, Haggai's enthusiasm for Temple restoration lasted throughout those years, constantly challenging the recalcitrant community to stay true to the task, though specific information about his role over that intervening period is all but lacking.

The Prophet Haggai

The primary character in the document that bears his name is generally referred to as 'the prophet Haggai'. Noted in Ezra 5.1 and 6.14 in this role as well, but lacking further personal information, Haggai is largely an unknown, even shadowy, personality. His name was not included in the list of returnees preserved in Ezra 2, but that does not automatically mean that he was not among those returnees who had been taken into exile. It seems less likely that he may have remained in Judaea after 587 BCE or was born in Judaea after the Babylonian invasion. For this commentary, Haggai was born in exile.

Assuming he was born in Babylonia, it is possible to imagine a little of his life in a Jewish enclave within a foreign cultural and religious environment. That he was insulated from foreign influences of various kinds would seem unlikely, and there would normally have been some level of foreign cultural input in his formation and sense of self, even in his understanding of Yahweh, the national God, who, in the view of many, had been humiliated by the 'victory' of the Babylonian gods in 587 BCE. However, it is clear from his support for the Deuteronomic ideology that he was on the more conservative end of the Israelite theological spectrum. What age he might have been in 538 BCE when given the chance to go to Jerusalem is unknown, but it is possible to picture him with his family and the several thousand other returnees walking slowly the hundreds of kilometres from regions of Babylonia to Jerusalem with all their belongings and a few animals, wondering what was ahead. Was he full of hope as echoed in his later promises? Had he already shown signs of a being a charismatic figure, similar to the ecstatic activity of those early prophets (1 Sam. 10.5; 2 Kgs 3.13-20)? When he saw Jerusalem for the first time, what was his reaction? What was his role, what did he do, other than get settled and housed, finding work like everyone else to support the family? Once identified as 'the prophet Haggai' by members of the community, what was his daily life like apart from those moments when publicly proclaiming God's message? Presumably, he lived a 'normal' life, but what was that? Was he a farmer, a day labourer, or an artisan of some kind? How did he provide for himself and a possible family? Being recognized as a prophet did not mean that this was a full-time task, doing nothing else than waiting for some revelation from God, then speaking out. How often was he overcome with the impulse to speak out?

Were the four occasions here dated the only occasions on which Haggai spoke, or are they simply a summary of his constant appeals to the community? Surely he spoke often about those matters that consumed him, each time adapting his presentation to differing and changing circumstances, as is common in the oral world. Oral presentations are adaptations of a theme built around keywords and patterns, not on a fixed and unvarying text, so the one version we have in the written document represents just one of multiple deliveries, now as a finalized form. Furthermore, Haggai's approach to his audience is characterized as indirect, asking questions and calling for those opposite to 'consider', or reflect, rather than confronting them in a more threatening manner. His language is more quiescent than the thunderings of a man like Isaiah (see Isa. 3.16-17, 24-26 etc.).

One element that stands out in what can be ascertained of Haggai's concerns is that he focused on religious matters more than on social and ethical issues. He was no Amos or Micah! Haggai's primary concern was for priestly issues such as the 'house of the Lord', urging that it be reinstated, an undertaking that he believed would, as a consequence, assure the community of better harvests. He was also concerned about torah, of people being 'clean' and about food taboos. Importantly, at no point does Haggai in this document accuse the people of sin, of moral failure, of injustice or lack of compassion for those disadvantaged, even if they were more heavily impacted by the drought and food shortages. His focus was the Temple and its store of treasures; but surprisingly, perhaps, he makes no mention of any cultic purpose for the rebuilding, either before or during the building work. Did Haggai have a vision for the Temple other than as a place where God in general terms 'could be honoured' (1.8)?

Reading what the editor has reported about the prophet and his concerns raises many questions to which one would like to have some firm answer in order to humanize the prophet, to enable one to 'meet' the man behind the screen, but, unfortunately, he will remain largely a remote character, a prophet formed in the Deuteronomic mold, the antithesis of Jonah, for example, and what some have regarded as an uninteresting man with a mundane message.

On Haggai, Zerubbabel and Joshua

The three central characters in Haggai are the prophet Haggai himself, the 'governor' Zerubbabel, and the high priest Joshua. Although precise information is very limited, we can assume that all three were born in Babylonia and grew up there until making their way to Judaea. As noted above, the circumstances in which one is raised can have a lasting impact on one's worldview and sense of identity, while 'foreign' cultural contexts can reshape the way one thinks and feels. Individuals react to challenging influences differently—some appreciate, then accept that new perspective, allowing it to enrich their understanding of self and the other, while some reject it and harden their resistance to all outside influences. Haggai clearly exemplified this latter group, grounded in his dependence on Deuteronomic theology, a perspective in which whatever happens in the community, in the natural world, in the international arena, was read in terms of divine intervention (see below). Ezra also belonged to this cohort, sharing these same views (Ezra 10.1-5), so one can be certain that within the returning community there were many whom one might regard as Deuteronomic 'hardliners'.

Zerubbabel was born and raised in Babylon and, despite his probable Davidic heritage, must have become known to the incoming Persian authorities as one Jewish leader who was sympathetic to more international interests and sufficiently amenable for Darius to appoint him as the primary authority figure, the 'governor', of Judaea. We need to see him as a figure of influence in the Jewish exilic community, as well as open and acceptable to the interests of Persian authorities, though specific details of his background are lacking. Zerubbabel's Akkadian name, Zerbabilu, indicates something of the level of adaptation that his Jewish family had made to Babylonian culture; he was what is known these days as a 'third culture kid', open to the wider world, a man able to walk the fine line between a narrow nationalistic view such as found in Deuteronomy and that offered by 'the other'. This fact must be taken into account when assessing his subsequent role and work in Jerusalem, especially in his interaction with Haggai, whose perspective was much more narrow.

Zerubbabel's appointment was as *peḥâ* of Judaea; translated generally as 'governor', it was a specific Persian term for one who was deputized to represent the Persian Empire in its various provinces. What is especially significant about his appointment is that it marked an end in a formal sense to the notion of kingship and the kingdom within ancient Israel; it highlighted the transition of power from the inherited throne, as it had been in the southern kingdom of Judah, to an appointed authority figure. Judaea from 520 BCE onward entered a new phase in which each new civil leader was under the authority of a foreign empire—first, that of Persia, then that of Greece and later of Rome. The promise of an 'eternal' covenant with the house of David, however, did not come to an end in the mind of many while ever there was present a descendant of the Davidic house, such as Zerubbabel may well have been. This was evident in the hope expressed by Haggai in the closing verses (2.20-23). How widespread this lingering hope of a Davidic return was is uncertain, but one should not necessarily think that it was universal.

Joshua was appointed high priest by the Persian (religious?) authorities, who were also responsible for Zerubbabel's appointment as governor. He, like Zerubbabel, must have been considered a 'safe' person to be assigned such a key posting, having gained the trust of Darius's officials, or he would not have been appointed to his representative position. According to a note in Ezra 10.18, he and his family had made adjustments to living biculturally in Babylonia. Joshua, perhaps surprisingly for a religious leader, was one of those in whose family were men who had married foreign wives, indicating a rejection of the narrow strictures imposed by Deuteronomy. Joshua's appointment, though unexplained, was a sure sign that the anti-foreign or exclusivist ideology of Deuteronomy had not impacted him to the extent that he was considered unsuitable to receive his assignment as high priest. We can presume that Joshua was known as open to Persian religious and cultural ideas, rather than being overly protective of any narrow Jewish religious views. In this he was fated to come into conflict with Haggai, and the editor reflects this by slowly writing Joshua out of his report. On the other hand, Zechariah appears to find Joshua more significant than Zerubbabel (Zech. 6.11-14).

No matter what other attributes Joshua and Zerubbabel may have demonstrated, their cultural and religious openness did not sit well with Haggai. While the depth or extent of foreign influence on the two leaders at the cultural and religious level is not measurable, they clearly attracted Persian interest such that both were given significant assignments. At the same time, their acceptability to the Persian hierarchy would be judged negatively by those of the Deuteronomic worldview, such as Haggai and Ezra. That clearly was a major factor in the prophet's view that the two were jointly responsible for what he saw as a failing in Jerusalem. The matter of housing, which was under Zerubbabel's order, and that of Temple repair, which should have been Joshua's concern, brought the prophet into conflict with them. This animosity or theological difference lies deep within the report of Haggai's message.

Aramaic or Hebrew?

A question rarely asked is Which language did Haggai use when addressing his audiences? While the report by Haggai's editor is in Hebrew, over the period of their exile the Jewish community had adapted culturally and linguistically to the point that the common language from this time on was Aramaic. Undoubtedly, Hebrew was still the language remembered by many, and it was especially evident during regular Jewish festivals when the traditional stories were recited; this can be seen in the postexilic documents and books that are in Hebrew. However, Hebrew was no longer the language of the people (see Ezra 4.8–6.18; Neh. 8.1-9). We may not be able to conclude with certainty which language Haggai used in the reported speeches, but if he was to communicate with the people on the broader scale, and with the two leaders who clearly had become acculturated to life in Babylon, he would have needed to address them in Aramaic. It was the editor who subsequently wrote the report in Hebrew. Are any of the minor difficulties in the current text of Haggai attributable to the process of transferring Haggai's ideas from one language to the other? Is this one reason why the Haggai text shows a non-traditional use of the basic messenger form for presenting his oracles? (See Appendix A below.)

Prophetic Insight

Unlike other prophetic books, there is no mention in Haggai of the manner in which the prophet received the information from the Lord that he was commissioned to pass on. The expression found in more traditional books, namely 'the word of the Lord (came) to X', is often followed by reference to how the message was acquired—e.g. Hab. 1.1, an 'oracle that ... Habakkuk saw'. So also Micah. Nahum 1.1 describes itself as a vision, likewise Ezekiel and Obadiah. Auditions and dreams were also claimed as sources of revelation to the prophets as they surveyed domestic and international matters. The formula *'Thus says the Lord'* and the closing *'says the Lord'* that bracket so many of the written prophetic speeches and oracles are not part of the content of the prophet's speech but of the editorial framework. However, for many readers the formulas are viewed as literally accurate statements of the process of inspired revelation without which the prophet would have little or nothing to say. The intent of the formula is to assert that the message is of divine origin, so it is of unquestioned authority; those addressed are required to acknowledge the prophet's credentials as a genuine prophet who speaks on behalf of God.

While prophetic books make much of the claim that what the prophets say is indeed received directly from God, in many cases consisting of the actual words the prophet should use (see Deut. 18.18-22), it is possible to overemphasize or exaggerate divine revelation as the prophet's source, as though the prophets spoke only what they were instructed to say. For example, Haggai is presented in the document that bears his name simply as a 'messenger', a conveyor of concerns and demands that originate with God, seeming to imply that he was little more than a ventriloquist's doll. However, the prophets were much more than conveyors of someone else's ideas and thoughts, as the varied or individualized prophetic materials illustrate well; many were keen observers of their society and times. They became courageous critics of national and communal failings that troubled them personally and about which they felt compelled to speak. As they encountered and reflected on the situations that confronted the community daily, they were driven to address particular conditions and arrangements that they themselves saw as unjust or unfair, such as the oppression of widows and orphans, of the poor and those disadvantaged; they called out religious laxity, unmasked hypocrisy, injustice and dishonest dealings because they themselves were affronted by them. Amos's attack on 'You cows of Bashan ... who oppress the poor and crush the needy' (Amo 4.1) did not need any special divine revelation for the prophet to be aware of and deeply offended by what he saw was wrong in Israel's northern kingdom. All that the prophets needed was a conscience and courage to speak out! Sensitivity to one's community and its situation, a personal vision for a better world, a community that valued justice and compassion and was faithful to its sense of being a community under God was what was required of any person to be recognized as a prophet, one also armed with the courage to speak out.

There is no need to see these two perspectives on prophetic sources as binary opposites, for it is far more likely that the reality as to prophetic insights and plain speaking lies somewhere between the two. In the case of Haggai, it is very likely that we are witness to the prophet's deep personal concern for the Temple restoration, given its centrality in Deuteronomy, along with his disappointment at Joshua the high priest's failure to effect the rebuilding; it was time, he believed, to set new priorities, and for him the Temple rebuild was an essential part of that. His concern may be traced to his Deuteronomic ideology, namely the importance of a sacred space in the place God had chosen to reside, and it was probably much more this personal concern that lay behind his challenge to the community to have the Temple rebuilt. To regard his message as stemming solely from a momentary flash of divine revelation, as seemingly implied in 1.1, is to read the report as literally factual rather than as an editor's *pro forma* account, and to be unduly influenced by the traditional phrases such as the 'the word of the Lord' and 'says the Lord', used in written documents.

Further evidence for the inner or personal element in prophetic challenges to the community is seen in that Haggai already knew well the answers to the questions about clean and unclean matters he was told to seek from the priests (2.10-13); these issues that dominated much of Israel's religious life were well understood by the community and did not require divine prodding for Haggai to gain the information or clarification he was ordered to request. Any understanding one might apply to the phrase 'the word of the Lord' as a prophet's one and only source of his message needs to consider it more carefully in light of the prophet's own insights and opinions, the personally held values that drove his mission.

When it came to making promises to their audiences, prophets frequently resorted to exaggeration, to hyperbole, to speak of a new set of circumstances that awaited those who would heed the warnings given. The promises may have encouraged and given hope, but more often than not, what they promised—defeat of all enemies, riches pouring in from the nations acknowledging Israel's God, peace for evermore—as did the promises of Haggai, raises problems when they were not fulfilled in the manner spoken of (see Deut. 18.22). Attributing these unfulfilled promises to God's revelation inevitably leads to questioning whether the promises were actually from God. Many prophetic promises are better regarded as arising from within the prophet's own concerns, as much more an expression of his deep personal hope and longing for the immediate future. That they were rarely, if ever, so fulfilled was the reality.

As for the future orientation of the prophetic word, the exaggerated language adopted and the failure of so many promises to be realized has led some readers to retain a literal reading of the words but then to project them into a distant future, to expand their compass beyond the prophet's immediate audience, and beyond anything that might have been in the mind of the individual prophet. Such a reading strategy depends on a preconceived view of the prophetic word that is not generic to the time and culture. The prophetic word was addressed to the prophet's contemporary audience, its time frame more immediate. What was the point in a prophet speaking in 520 BCE to his immediate audience if his message is actually about events hundreds of years into the future, long after their passing? Projecting prophetic statements and promises into the distant future because not seen to be realized immediately reverses the way in which the Jewish tradition read its Scriptures; it read texts backward. The later rabbis searched their texts to link their present to their past, re-reading even the most indirect references found there in a way that tied their present to the past and enlightened their 'now'; it was a reading strategy called *midrash*. This reverse reading has nothing to do with later 'fulfilment' but everything to do with affirming a subsequent generation's valued links with its past.

Literary Features of Haggai

The Haggai editor has created four brief narrative reports based on messages said to have been received by the prophet over four months in 520

BCE. (See 'Dating Haggai' below.) They show what he knew of Haggai's original messages via a narrative in third person, so the editor was at some remove from Haggai, as is evident when he refers to Yahweh as 'their God' (1.12-14). As third-person narrative, Haggai is closer to a book like Jonah than it is to other prophetic works. A number of literary features can be identified within each of the four reports.

Readers of the current text of Haggai will recognize several inserts, narrative breaks, repetitions and truncated reports that, in places, hinder a smooth reading from one verse or one topic to the next. From this perspective the document is not a coherent narrative but more a collection of diverse oral messages largely to do with the Temple rebuilding, set within reports that are chronologically, if not logically, arranged over the four specified dates. There are at least two matters in this report that leave a reader with questions arising from what appear to be incomplete texts: e.g. 2.10-14 ends abruptly without any clarification as to what was involved in the prophet's declaration that everything the people have done was 'unclean'; and in 2.20-23 the report of Zerubbabel's elevation to power over the kingdoms was an announcement unrelated to any of Haggai's other concerns, lacking in specific context, and leaving the reader wondering about the real implications for Zerubbabel other than his being 'like a signet'.

Unlike the authors of many other prophetic works, Haggai's editor shows little or no use of traditional prophetic speech forms apart from the very basic messenger form. See Appendix A for a survey of the non-standard use of the basic form, *'Thus says the Lord, . . . says the Lord'*, that initiates and concludes many oracles throughout the prophetic collection. While there are fragments of Haggai's speeches quoted, the editor has chosen third-person narrative as the primary literary form for presenting the report on Haggai and for recording the popular reaction or response to Haggai's message.

As for specific features of Haggai's presentation, they are briefly noted here for later expansion:

1. Echoes of Deuteronomy's language use are clearly evident in Haggai's vocabulary with the use of three key terms—obey, bless, chosen (1.12; 2.19; 2.23)—and the ideology that surrounds them.
2. Inserts and breaks in the text hinder a smooth reading. For example, 1.8 interrupts the call to 'consider' in 1.7-9; the narrative 2.10-14 ends without explaining what makes the people and their work 'unclean'; in 2.17 the charge that the people did not 'return' to the Lord appears to be a gloss from Zechariah. These are each explained fully in the comments on the relevant verses: 1.8, 2.5cd, 2.17, and 2.19d.

3. The imperative to 'consider' past events (1.5, 7; 2.16) as well as the future (2.15, 18-19) portrays the key challenge Haggai makes to the leaders and people of Jerusalem. The call in each case follows a pattern, suggesting that each pair represents two slightly differing versions of the one call.
4. Contrasting adverbs 'much' and 'little' underpin the two versions of harvest failure (1.5-6, 7-9) in the opening report.
5. Questions as a means of challenging his hearers was the format chosen by the editor to present Haggai's encounters with his audience in each of the four dated messages (1.4; 2.3, 15-16, 18-19).
6. Hyperbole is central to Haggai's overall speech pattern as recorded. In Hag. 1.4 the prophet describes the people's houses in a manner that suggests they are quite splendid, perhaps paneled in wood, an expensive item in Judaea, in contrast to the desolate Temple ruin. The contrast is exaggerated for effect. He promises that the restored Temple will outshine the Solomonic Temple (2.8); that God will 'shake the heavens, and the earth, the sea and the dry land' (2.6), adding that he will also shake the nations so that they send treasures to Jerusalem for the adornment of the Temple (2.8); then he will destroy the nations and their armies (2.22). These were promises that were never, nor could ever be, realized in the manner described.
7. On two occasions the report uses the figure of 'shaking', whether of the cosmos or nations, to describe God's intervention on Judaea's behalf (2.6-9, 21-23). In both cases multiple examples of the concluding form *'says the Lord'* are inserted for emphasis.
8. Negatively, it is interesting that Haggai makes no reference to Jerusalem or the Temple, mimicking Deuteronomy. The Temple is simply 'the/this house'.

Haggai and Deuteronomy

I have concluded that Haggai was thoroughly dependent on the theology found in the Book of Deuteronomy, a book that has a long and complex history involving redaction or editorial processes that span a number of years. It is generally agreed that the final redaction of Deuteronomy took place over a period in the early years of the Babylonian exile. It was also during this period that what has become known as the Deuteronomistic History (DH)—Joshua, Judges, 1–2 Samuel and 1–2 Kings—was also worked on by scribes until reaching a final form, perhaps as early as 560 BCE. That history is the story of the people of Israel from their settlement in Canaan to the end of the two kingdoms, northern Israel and southern Judah, retold in light of the core values in Deuteronomy. It is not possible to be exact in matters of compilation and redaction over such long periods, but there is every good reason to accept that this is what took place, beginning with the central core, Deuteronomy 12–26, and then expanded. What one can say with certainty is that the DH reflects at many levels, especially the literary and theological levels, the language and thoughts that are central to the precepts and ideology of the book of Deuteronomy.

Deuteronomy expresses a strongly nationalistic viewpoint; it is about Israel seeing itself as God's chosen people, a people separate from all others because they had a unique covenant with Yahweh, their God, and lived in a land that Yahweh gave them (Ezra 9.12–10.15). That land, though occupied by other tribes at the time of the Israelites' arrival at the Jordan's eastern bank at the end of the Exodus journey, now belonged to Israel by virtue of Yahweh's gift, so those tribes who were currently in the land had to be driven out, with none spared. Genocide was justified because it was demanded by Yahweh in order to keep his people safe from alien religious values and to ensure long-term possession of the land (Deut. 7.1-11)! The true Israel was now defined as those who under Yahweh left Egypt in the Exodus, passed through the desert and then entered Canaan; this was an exclusive community. That status and relationship would remain so long as Israel was obedient to the Law, ensuring God's blessing. Israel's God was active in its life as well as in the international scene—punishing and rewarding—all this activity, according to the Deuteronomic viewpoint, being for the sole benefit of God's chosen people (Deut. 7.6). In Haggai, editor and prophet both are grounded in this tradition of exclusivity.

Haggai interprets the crisis facing the people of Judaea, namely the harvest failure, as the direct result of God's intervention, an intervention designed to impress upon the people that they should reprioritize and give themselves to Temple repair. His interpretation of the crop failure is rooted in an acceptance of the Deuteronomic ideology set out so clearly in Deut. 7.12-16; 28.20-24, 38-40. That God will 'strike' the people with hardship (2.17) is anticipated in the warning of Deut. 28.35, where it is only one of a range of verbs that speak of divine initiative inflicting disasters on a recalcitrant nation.

One point to bear in mind as one reads Haggai is that, according to the Deuteronomic viewpoint, it was Yahweh who had brought about the end of the kingdom of Judah and thus the destruction of Jerusalem, including especially of the Temple in 587 BCE (see 2 Kgs 24.2-4, 13; also Ezra 5.12). Ironically, the reason that the Temple site was lying in ruins in 520 can be traced back to that earlier alleged divine intervention, using the Babylonian army as his agent of destruction and judgment. Now, Haggai says, God wants it re-established!

The core ideology of Deuteronomy is not confined to the DH but can be found widespread in the messages of prophets such as Jeremiah and Hosea. It was one enduring theological view that marked Israelite culture and religion over an extended period before, during and after the exile, so it is not surprising to find that a prophet like Haggai was committed to its basic tenets, ideas about God, God's activity, sacred places, Torah, the land of promise, and Israel as God's chosen people. Haggai uses three keywords typical of Deuteronomy—obey (1.12), bless (2.19) and chosen (2.23)—another indicator of his direct link with its overall language, worldview and theology.

Authorship

Who then wrote the Haggai document? It is not a question that can be answered simplistically, other than to say, it was not Haggai. Some would say that it is altogether the wrong question to ask, the reason being that so much happens in an oral culture between an original pronouncement by a prophet or storyteller, its repetition, transmission within the community, and its eventual recording. Many hands have had input into the written form of Haggai as finalized by the editor. His report has brought together a number of traditions about Haggai and about what he spoke of, not just once but on numerous occasions, issues that were no doubt also discussed by the community throughout Judaea, especially by those who failed to see the urgency or importance of what concerned the prophet. The prophet's challenge to the community was not like a simple one-off sermon but rather a live debate in which what he said would have led to discussions not only in Jerusalem but throughout the province. The challenge to rebuild the Temple would have made serious demands on people's time, their labour and finances; hence it would have been much discussed.

Haggai, like most of his contemporaries, would almost certainly have been illiterate and not written anything himself, but would have repeated his messages, adapting them slightly to fit the occasion and circumstances of his audiences. It is in the very nature of the oral process that slight variations in the specific contents of the prophet's challenge would emerge. There is evidence within the edited text that variant versions of Haggai's message were incorporated by the editor without any attempt to unify them (see notes on 1.5-6 and 1.7-11). What the editor as scribe has done is to collate and make his report from all the materials available to him. At some subsequent point, the report has been written on parchment and stitched into the Scroll as the tenth document in what became the Scroll of the Twelve.

Editorial Contributions in Prophetic Writings

So much of the prophetic literature is characterized by the use of an extensive range of literary forms and tropes; it is the literate editor who provided these established forms such as *'Thus says the Lord'* and *'says the Lord'* that are attached to the written prophetic utterances. The fact that these forms are common to all the prophetic writings is a sign that they derive from literate editors schooled in their use. The literary forms are well established, fixed and wooden, whereas an oral presentation was much more dynamic, energetic, occasionally marked by angry outbursts such as 'Hear (listen up) you people' (e.g. Amos 8.4; Mic. 1.2; 6.1). Committing them to writing fixes them in a non-fluid form.

In the commentary that follows it is assumed that the entire work in its present form comes from the hands of an editor (or community of editors) who shared the prophet's ideology, his Deuteronomic perspective. The extent to which Haggai was personally involved in the recording of these elements of his message, given that the message and popular responses are essentially narrative about him, would point to, at most, a minimal role for the prophet himself. What we are reading is a third-person report of traditions circulating about a prophet whose (apparently) very brief mission highlighted concerns in Jerusalem in 520 BCE. Depending on how long after the events of 520 BCE it was before the editor managed to compile this report (see below), it is possible that Haggai was no longer on the scene when it became available, so editing was entirely at the whim of the editor, who provided not only the dates but, more importantly, generated the narrative connecting the prophet's calls that had circulated in the community, and in this process he became the document's real author.

Dating Haggai

The editor's narrative that is the 'book' of Haggai concluded a period of oral transmission of the prophet's messages, sealing them in written form. That written report could not have been completed until after the final dated message was received, shared, talked about and finally edited some time after the date given in 2.20, namely the 24th day of the ninth month, or the eighteenth of December, 520 BCE. How long after Haggai's initial reception of the messages it was before the editor completed his report is unclear, but there would have been the lapse of some considerable time. One can assume that the editor, representing the process itself, was not constantly accompanying the prophet and recording immediately what he had to say; rather, what he has recorded was based on oral accounts circulating within the community. In the case of the final message (2.20-23), the prophet is said to have delivered that message to Zerubbabel privately, so how the editor came to know of its contents is again one of those uncertainties.

While the dates on which the messages were received are given, the possible date for the final report is unknown, but a reasonable length of time should be allowed for the process that culminated in the present written document. Despite the fact that there is no indication in the present Haggai text that the Temple rebuilding may have been completed in 516 BCE (see Ezra 6.15), what one can say with a degree of confidence is that the 'book' may have reached a final written form just prior to that date, perhaps between 518 and 517 BCE. This fact may have some implications for the 'promise' component of Haggai's messages in terms of the inflow of treasures for the Temple and the anticipated role of Zerubbabel; there is no textual evidence here as to the realization of either of these promises.

Haggai and its Theological Ideas

Deuteronomic Foundation

The theological or ideological foundation of Haggai is the worldview set out most clearly in the book of Deuteronomy, a book that represents Israel's self-understanding as an exclusive community in covenant with its God, Yahweh (Deut. 29.1-9). It represents the religious views of a significant cohort from pre-exilic days that continued within postexilic Judaism. It was this cohort whose rigid and simple view of blessings for obeying and curses for disobeying the Law as given (Deut. 28.1-24) retold the story of Israel's journey from settlement in Canaan (Joshua–Judges) to the end of the kingdoms (1 Samuel–2 Kings), that is, the Deuteronomistic History (DH), using its distinctive criteria and couching it all in terms and phrases that are readily identifiable as peculiar to this source.

Within this Deuteronomic perspective, the blessings God offers those who live according to Torah, are identified as material benefits—for example, many children, good harvests, bountiful livestock, freedom from illness, success in various enterprises, including war (see Deut. 7.12-16)—as are the curses for disobedience, namely drought, famine, few children, defeat in battle and so on. Haggai clearly accepted and applied this Deuteronomic worldview, and from this perspective attributed the current difficulties faced in Judaea directly to divine intervention brought about by their failure to rebuild the Temple. Haggai took his community to task for prioritizing their own needs over that of the 'this house' (Temple) and its God. It suggests that Haggai's vision for the Temple, rather than being an end in itself, was as a means to an end, namely to remove the threat to the community's livelihood; if they rebuilt the Temple, God would, by implication, restore the food and other material benefits that were now lacking. Haggai's is therefore, along with Deuteronomy, a theology in which God weaponizes environmental conditions, withdrawing rainfall and fertility from crops and other agricultural production, causing physical hardship, as means of punishing an entire population, and even the animals, for what he views as a communal failing. Drought and harvest failure, according to Haggai, can mean only one thing: the people have offended God. Such a simple explanation for a very complex problem.

Haggai used an indirect means of delivering this message rather than one of confrontation; he did so by questioning the people's choices. He did not accuse them of breaking laws or of moral failure; Haggai did not accuse his audience of 'disobedience', a charge normally made in other prophetic texts when highlighting perceived failings. What he did do was to apply Deuteronomic principles to the current condition of harvest shortfall, arriving at his conclusion that it resulted from a failure to honour God with a 'house' in the place that he had chosen to dwell or 'put his name', a place fit for God's enjoyment. From the reality of the current situation, an effect, Haggai has argued a cause. This simple conclusion stems directly from his view of Yahweh, and of the way he believes Yahweh interacts with not only his people but with the natural world as well.

Haggai and the Mosaic Covenant

Haggai reflects the Mosaic covenant tradition, as seen in Deuteronomy 29, a relationship Israel believed was first offered by Yahweh at Sinai then supplemented in Moab prior to entering 'the land'. It promised success 'in everything you do' (Deut. 29.9), conditional upon observing the covenant's requirements but threatening the devastation of the land of those who 'turn away'. Their land 'will be afflicted, the soil burned out with sulphur and salt ... unable to support any vegetation' (Deut. 29.14-29). The covenant's conditions for receiving the blessings offered were dependent on the whole community's obedience (see Exod. 19.1-5; Deut. 5.1-5; 7.1-6; 29.1-29). Haggai's message is fully coordinated with this tradition though he does not at any point specifically accuse his audience of disobedience or sin.

Haggai's Concept of the Divine

Haggai's preferred way of referring to God was as 'Lord of hosts', a title that appears to predate the Israelite monarchy. The earliest reference is to be found in 1 Sam. 1.3, with the name linked to the Shiloh sanctuary. Israel's relationship with its God was founded on the special covenant established between them at Sinai (or Horeb, according to Deuteronomy) in which Israel was said to become 'his people' and he 'your God' (Deut. 29.4,

13). The 'hosts' over which this their God is Lord refers, in the primary instance, to an army or to warfare (Exod. 7.4; 12.17), but it has an expanded figurative usage that describes the 'hosts' of heaven, the sun, the moon and the stars (Deut. 4.19; 17.3), and may also be used of the countless angels as divine messengers (Isa. 24.21), including the heavenly hosts of Job 1.

While 'Lord of hosts' does seem to be a title that appears more often in the later prophetic works, it is interesting to note that Haggai chose that title in particular, giving the impression that his perception of God and the way God works was as one with vast power, such as is able to 'shake' the cosmos and the nations. For Haggai, then, he viewed and spoke of Yahweh as Lord in militaristic terms. Along with this feature, it is important to observe that Haggai makes *no* reference to divine compassion, love, rescue/salvation, loyalty, hope or divine gifts of any kind; and the two references to the divine presence in 1.13 and 2.4-5 seem more to be formal inserts than powerful statements of a gracious and caring divine figure. So, what kind of a God is Haggai's God? Since Haggai does not make any direct reference to divine traits or character, we are left with the general military imagery of God's leading the hosts. His God was hardly the kind so revered and honoured by other prophets for whom love, compassion and readiness to forgive at least balance any other traits such as divine anger, disappointment and punishment.

Religious Not Moral Crusade

Haggai's primary concerns revolved around religious rather than moral or social justice issues. In this respect Haggai differed markedly from those other prophets such as Hosea, Amos and Micah for whom those latter issues were central. Perhaps this focus arose from the specific nature of Haggai's mission, his personal desire to see the Temple reinstated and playing its role once again in the life of the people. Whether Haggai did have an interest in justice and related social issues ultimately cannot be decided simply on the basis of what little is left of his memory. On the other hand, what he was remembered for was that narrow religious concern. No further information about him and his witness was reported or included in other contemporary sources.

Yahweh and the Natural World

When Haggai referred to the crisis facing the people in 520 BCE, the lack of food, the failure of crops, and lack of income to sustain their lives, he expressed it in terms of divine punishment. It was God who called for a drought and sent mildew that decimated crops; it was God who deliberately 'struck' them with this harvest shortfall. Founded upon the Deuteronomic notion of blessing for obedience and curses for disobedience, Haggai showed his acceptance of this concept of God as one who weaponizes nature for his own ends; the natural world was for Haggai an instrument in God's dealings with humanity, and especially for punishing his people Israel. Seeing God the Creator at work in and behind the natural cycle of drought and plenty was a central item in Haggai's belief system.

Yahweh and World Powers

Just as Haggai saw God active in the natural world, he saw God working out his purposes in the life of the nations. Haggai presents his God as master or lord not only of Israel's life, but as Lord of the Universe, the one who can 'shake' the entire cosmos and the world of nations. This universal and cosmic activity was said to bring disaster on the enemies of Israel, and as enemies of Israel, they were by definition, enemies of its God. The ultimate goal of this divine activity among the nations was to effect a benefit or blessing for God's people in Judaea and Jerusalem (2.6, 21-22); it is an unashamedly nationalistic claim that God serves one's own national values and interests. While this aspect of the divine mission was not elaborated in terms of how God actually 'shook' the nations, the message was clear: Haggai understood God as a power whose primary interest and purpose were in working to bring benefit and glory to his people in Judaea.

Proclamations of the defeat of enemies in Hag. 2.6-8, 22 were, like all political messages, directed at the local community audience; the nations never got to hear, nor was it intended that they should hear, these promises of their impending defeat and humiliation. Isaiah (chs. 13–23), Jeremiah (chs. 46-51), and Obadiah and their collected oracles against foreign nations, were more concerned about denouncing the nations' abuse of power and injustice, and their being punished for past actions, rather than claiming a divine intervention that was of future benefit to the Judaeans. It is also clearly different from the view expressed in Isa. 10.5-11 in which Assyria was regarded as God's instrument for judgment against Israel itself.

The Temple in Haggai's Plan

The 'house of the Lord', Haggai's preferred description of the Temple, was for Haggai a central plank in the Judaean relationship with Yahweh. It was vital to have this visible and glorious 'house' for Yahweh to reside in and enjoy (1.8; 2.9), a potent symbol or reminder that Yahweh was 'with them'. Haggai's focus initially was the rebuilding of the Temple, its silver and gold decorative components, along with its function as the treasury. This was the 'glory' of which he spoke. Haggai believed that this was where the peoples' work priorities should lie—expressed as a concern for Yahweh rather than for self. Once God's house had been restored, then the community would truly become whole again with Yahweh resident among them. Now that there was no king, it was the Temple that could become a focal point of the community's identity. What Haggai seems not to have been particularly concerned about was its actual religious function, its cultic role, the place where sacrifices could be offered, for Haggai makes no mention of any cultic activity when advocating the rebuilding. Having it rebuilt as God's dwelling was his primary objective, and one can perhaps assume that with that task begun, he expected the people's livelihood to be turned around—as though beginning the task of rebuilding in itself would change their fortunes and end the current crisis.

Day of the Lord
On one occasion, 2.23, the final verse of the 'book', Haggai uses the phrase 'on that day', citing the formal phrase associated with the notion of the Day of the Lord (see below for details). It was a formula used primarily by the prophets to express Israel's expectations for the future. It was, of course, not a literal 'day' but an occasion, a moment in the future, when God was expected to act in some manner, be it in decisive judgment or in compassionate rescue. Here in Haggai the single use carries the prophet's hope for a resurgence in Zerubbabel's leadership, his authority conferred by Yahweh rather than by the current Persian overlords.

Haggai 1

Outline of Contents

1.1-15a	First Message: August 29, 520 BCE
1.1-2	Editor's Introduction
1.3-11	Haggai's Call to Rebuild the Temple
1.5-6	'Consider . . .' I
1.7-11	'Consider . . .' II
1.12-15a	The People's Positive Response
1.15b–2.9	Second Message: October 17, 520 BCE
	The Glory of the Rebuilt Temple Assured
2.10-19	Third Message: December 18, 520 BCE
2.10-14	Priests Rule on the Law of Holiness; Haggai Applies the Principle
2.15-19	Two Calls to Reflect on the Future
2.15-17	'Consider . . .' III
2.18-19	'Consider . . .' IV
2.20-23	Fourth Message: December 18, 520 BCE
	Haggai Promises a Future for Zerubbabel

Structure

The structure of this short document is clear and simple, based on the four specific dates on which the prophet received commands to address the two leaders in particular, Zerubbabel and Joshua, and the Judaean community in general. The dates are provided by the redactor, linking with some presumed official but external Persian record.

    Haggai, the first of the known postexilic prophets, addressed the community in Jerusalem with what are now four messages on issues that concerned the prophet. They were (1) the people's reluctance to begin Temple renovations because priority had been given to personal housing, a priority that Haggai criticized as being the reason for the current harvest shortfall (1.1-15a); (2) the disappointment Haggai felt at the quality of the work done once Temple restoration had begun, followed by a promise of treasures from the nations to embellish the building (1.15b–2.9); (3) the priestly definition of 'clean' and 'unclean' and how Haggai then interpreted and applied their explanation to the current crisis (2.10-14) with two calls to 'consider' where matters stood with the community (2.15-19); (4) the promise of victory over enemies and the elevation of Zerubbabel, the chosen one (2.20-23).

However, within this simple structure there lies the question of the overall unity of its contents. Beginning with the view that it was the final editor who gathered and set the material within the four dates, one can accept that a measure of unity derives from that. What they do not share is a logical or thematic connection as might be expected in a narrative context. For example, the call to 'consider' in 1.7-9 is broken apart by the interruption of 1.8, which has nothing to do with any reflection on the crisis of the moment. Also, the order to ask questions of the priests in 2.10-14 is clearly an isolated unit unrelated to the surrounding material, as is the final report in 2.20-23. My reading will also question the addition of notes in 2.17b and 2.19c as insertions that are unexpected.

These elements suggest that Haggai, the document, is a report in which the editor has assembled a variety of loosely related stories about Haggai's encounters with the two leaders and with the people regarding Temple reconstruction, placing them within a time frame of several months in 520 BCE. The arrangement is not haphazard, but certainly the editor has not made a major effort to harmonize the component parts. The inclusion of what I argue are two similar versions of oral accounts in 1.5-6, 1.7-9, and 2.15-17, 2.18-19, together with a quote in 2.17b, presumably from Zechariah, add to this reader's sense that the editor has constructed his report from available select material that he believed could be traced back to Haggai's brief ministry in 520 BCE.

1.1-15a First Dated Message

The editor introduces the report on Haggai's mission by providing a precise date on which Haggai received a message specifically intended for Zerubbabel the governor and for Joshua the high priest (1.1), but also indirectly incorporating the entire community. By referring to them generally as 'this people', the editor adds a dismissive or condescending tone. As the two leaders now resident in Jerusalem, Zerubbabel and Joshua were responsible for the civil and religious life of the community. Their appointment to these positions by the Persian authorities we can assume was politically motivated. Darius would not appoint as 'governor' or as high priest persons who did not promise allegiance and acceptance of the policy decisions he would impose on the Judaean province. Darius anticipated that both appointees would comply with and advance Persian interests. It was politically astute for the new King Darius to appoint Zerubbabel, a descendant of Shealtiel (1 Chron. 3.17-19), as governor, given his possible Davidic heritage, but he would surely have set strict limitations around any potential independence threat or challenge to Persian policy that any might associate with such an appointment. The editor in 1.2 presents the prophet and his message, identifying the issue that was Haggai's core concern—the delay in restoring the devastated Temple to its former glory.

For Zerubbabel, the civil leader, housing would have been one of many basic concerns, less so the Temple and activities associated with it, for those lay with Joshua, whose religious responsibility was to ensure that community life conformed with Torah, instructing the people in God's requirements. Presumably he also had a measure of responsibility for overseeing the restoration of the Temple building in preparation, eventually, for a full program of religious rituals, despite the fact that the text makes no mention of him in this role. How was it that the one responsible for the religious life of the community had not convinced people to prioritize the Temple revival? How was he regarded by the community? It would appear that Joshua was of little consequence to the editor, and this is reflected in the very minimal role he is given in the editorial report. And what of those many priests who returned with Joshua? In the 18 years since the returnees first began arriving, little had been done to restore the Temple in view of the greater perceived need to establish their livelihoods. Temple restoration was not a matter of such urgency, and the priests' normal concerns were irrelevant to the practical needs of the people, much to Haggai's despair. Tension over the issue was inevitable, with many having had their cultural and religious experience reshaped while in exile through years of foreign cultural and religious influence, of intermarriage with foreigners, and with serious residual questions about Yahweh's supposed universal power and commitment to those who claimed to be 'his people'. For many in this cohort, the need for a Temple restoration project under their current circumstances was not great, if needed at all. Jerusalem as a centre of Yahwistic worship had not been available to them for almost 60 years—and may not have been missed by many—so there was no urgency felt generally for Temple repair. Their priority for their own housing, however, was not an outright refusal to undertake Temple repair; it was merely a matter of present priorities—work on the Temple was not urgent. The exilic experience for many had resulted in a serious re-evaluation of past religious traditions centered around the Temple, and on returning to Jerusalem many saw no desperate need to reinstate what once had been so important, and Joshua had not persuaded them otherwise.

Having provided an introduction to the report, the editor refers again to the prophet's receipt of a message (1.3) and presents it via a rhetorical question (1.4) concerning the audience's priorities regarding time allocated to private housing rather than to Temple restoration work. There seems never to have been a question that the Temple would at some point be revived—just not yet. The rhetorical question did not need a voiced response as it was obvious that the community at large felt that the Temple work could wait; for them it really was appropriate to prioritize their own housing ahead of the Temple repair. In contrast, God's priority, according to Haggai, was not community housing but for God to have his own 'house' repaired. God's priority was what mattered to Haggai!

Haggai's way of responding to what he regarded as a recalcitrant community's priority differed from the direct condemnatory approach of other prophets who railed against their communities (e.g. Isa. 24.1-13; Jer. 23.1-4). He adopted a more indirect, perhaps more subtle, method; he invited them via a series of questions to think about their current domestic situation and its practical challenges. Haggai called all to 'consider' or reflect on the failed expectations for their new life in Jerusalem. The difficulties they had been facing, presumably for some time, were very real. The contrast between 'much' and 'little' in 1.6, 9 characterizes the reality of their situation; nothing measured up to what had been anticipated, and their hard work was barely rewarded. For some there would have been a sense of regret at having abandoned Babylonia to now encounter such hardship. For Haggai, however, there was an obvious and simple explanation for the current set of circumstances, a clear case of cause and effect; the problems encountered (effect) had a direct link with their failure to complete the Temple repair (cause). He attributed the dire situation the people faced to divine intervention (1.10-11), a God-induced drought that decimated all agricultural production—even the animals suffered—and for Haggai the hardship was assuredly the consequence of the Temple lying yet in ruins. Haggai's explanation for the people's hardship arose directly from his dependence on the kind of ideology that is explicit in the book of Deuteronomy (see 'Theological Ideas' in **Introduction**). But would his words provide any comfort?

The hardship described as current in Jerusalem needs to be acknowledged. Despite its earlier prominence as the kingdom of Judah in the Israelite story from 1000 to 587 BCE, Judaea was actually a remote and sparsely populated province, relatively poor, distant from the major roads that might connect Jerusalem to the rest of the region. This disadvantaged geographical situation, with limited land suited to agriculture, poor soils and unreliable rainfall, was climatically challenged and overshadowed by the more fertile and wealthier Samaritan region to its north; it was never the most inviting environment. Judaea had always been in danger of drought and famine because of its geographical location, so to hear of these elements adversely affecting the region in 522–520 BCE was unsurprising; people in the region of Judaea had for centuries lived with the constant threat of drought and crop failure. So, many would wonder why Haggai thought to connect this condition simply to the lack of progress on Temple rebuilding.

After challenging the community with his message for about three weeks, Haggai apparently elicited a response. The editor relates a positive reaction from the two leaders and from what is described as 'all the remnant of the people', a phrase used three times—in 1.12, 14 and 2.2. The latter phrase generally identifies some portion of a community as separate from others, in many cases referring to those who survived a crisis, so it may refer to those who had come back from Babylon, but it could well apply to those who survived the 587 destruction of Jerusalem and who had remained in place. The 'remnant' in this context may simply refer generally to that group who responded to Haggai's preaching. This remnant or limited cohort, along with their two leaders, being persuaded by Haggai's words, responded positively to Haggai's call. Their positive response was also attributed by the editor to divine intervention, inspiring their 'spirits', (Hebrew uses the word 'heart') enthusing all concerned, prompting them to act. Being assured by the prophet that the divine presence would abide with those who took his explanation to heart, the Temple rebuilding eventually got under way.

This first message is the edited narrative of an amazing turnaround in the attitude of Zerubbabel, Joshua and a group of supporters. Haggai 1.12-15a is an idealized story of the outcome of Haggai's challenge.

1.1-2 The Editor's Introduction

1.1 In the second year of King Darius, on the first day of the sixth month, the word of the Lord was delivered by the prophet Haggai to Zerubbabel son of Shealtiel, governor of Judaea, and to Joshua son of Jehozadak, the high priest.

1.2 This is what the Lord of hosts said: 'This people have said that the time has not yet come for the house of the Lord to be (re)built.'

The editor opens in 1.1 nominating a specific date, the first day of the sixth month of the second year of the reign of the Persian King Darius I, that is, 520 BCE. During the exile the Jews came to adopt the Babylonian lunar calendar that began in the spring, so the sixth month would correspond roughly with August/September in the northern hemisphere. It is said to be the date Haggai 'received' the message he was to convey, not that he necessarily communicated it then and there. There is no way that the dates supplied can be verified independently, nor are we certain as to why the editor saw such precision about the dates to be an important element in his narrative. However, in 2 Kings 25, when reporting the final events in the life of the former southern kingdom, a similar dating profile is used (25.1, 3, 8, 27), so one can assume that there was some reliable record behind the dates given. Specifying dates as the editor has done leads some to assert that the function of dating in ancient documents was to underscore the truth value of an event and to emphasize the authenticity of its message. While this may be so, such a conclusion is often more a projection by modern scholars concerned with biblical historicity than one based on contemporary evidence, and a failure to acknowledge the confessional or political purpose in the recording of traditions that may well exaggerate the importance of the person or event so claimed. What can be considered more relevant here is that the August/September period was the time for harvesting a number of crops, a point that relates directly to Haggai's message in 1.6, 10-11 concerning the harvest shortfall.

The specific day and month in the year in which the message was said to have been received has been calculated to be the twenty-ninth of August, 520 BCE. The date itself is largely immaterial, for it points only to the 'reception' of a message and says nothing about its dissemination. The four dated entries are provided by the editor and are not integral to the prophetic message *per se*, so their function within the report is not related to its content. That message itself summarizes the issue Haggai was to raise, and over the next period of time he would seek out Zerubbabel, seek out Joshua, speak with groups and individuals here and there throughout the territory, challenging each with the call to rebuild the Temple. It was so important a message for Haggai that he would have spoken many times in various places throughout Judaea, pressing his case in words and forms that were appropriate to his various audiences. How many times did Haggai confront Zerubbabel or question Joshua or any other significant person? Surely not just once, as a 'flat' or unimaginative reading might suggest. If Haggai was recognized as a prophet worthy of a hearing, his calls would have been discussed by the community at large. A prophet spoke passionately of whatever he or she felt compelled to say, and did so on many occasions, adapting their words to the setting and circumstances while using keywords and phrases together with structural elements to aid his presentation and the hearers' retention of the message. What we have in this edited introduction is just a brief summary of the issue that burdened Haggai.

Although there is potentially a link between the given date and the annual harvest season generally, and thus with the crisis facing the community, that relationship cannot be applied to more than the first message; for the other dated messages, any seasonal connection is moot. However, specific dating such as was provided by the editor of Haggai was also a feature adopted by the editor of Zechariah (1.1; 7.1), suggesting that using such a form of introduction was a new development, replacing the citing of regnal periods typical of earlier prophetic documents when Israel was ruled by kings—see Hos. 1.1; Amos 1.1. Whether the Haggai editor was also responsible for editing Zechariah 1–8 is often discussed but is a matter of debate. Zechariah's editor has also added the name of the Jewish month to his dates.

The two leaders addressed by Haggai were each being blamed for the current situation with regard to the community's priorities in Jerusalem; the rest of the community is only secondarily implicated, but the responsibility for the priorities chosen lay ultimately with the two leaders. Haggai obviously regarded Zerubbabel and Joshua as offering poor leadership, especially so in the case of Joshua, the high priest, of whom more should have been expected; he it was who was accountable by his silence, if not by direct opposition, for the general reluctance to undertake the immediate repair of the Temple. As Zerubbabel was the civil leader, one of whose responsibilities was housing, there was potential for a conflict between him and Joshua. Assuming Joshua had tried, he had absolutely failed to convince Zerubbabel and the people of the importance of Temple rebuilding. Haggai's message sought to re-arrange Zerubbabel's priorities while criticizing Joshua's failure to encourage Temple repair as a top priority.

The standard phrase 'word of the Lord' is a short-hand form appended to records of messages said to have been received by prophets; the phrase implied that the message was derived from an external source. (The concept itself, however, should not be confined to prophetic materials alone.) Each of the Old Testament prophetic documents uses the form extensively as a fixed literary form. The shared use of literary forms down through the centuries suggests that it was the editors of the written documents who were largely responsible for developing them and then putting the prophets' oral presentations into one or more of the required formats. An opening phrase *'Thus says the Lord . . .'* and then a closing phrase *'. . . says the Lord'*, the so-called messenger form, was a form suitable within a written document, but in the oral and original setting of a prophet's presentation, a more colloquial phrase can be imagined as more appropriate, such as 'Listen, you leaders' (e.g. Mic. 1.2; 3.1 etc.). The phrase 'word of the Lord' is ambiguous: the Hebrew genitive form *dbr yhwh* can mean a word from the Lord (subjective genitive)—the sense widely attributed to it—or, a word about or concerning the Lord (objective genitive). (It is a similar case with the phrase 'the love of God', meaning one's love for God, or the love that God shows toward one.) The 'word of the Lord' phrase can also be applied generically to the content of visions and auditions. While a number of the prophets are described as seeing visions (Amos 1.1; Mic. 1.1), or hearing audibly the message they are to pass on (Hos. 1.1; Zech. 1.18), there is no mention of the medium by which Haggai came to know what message he was to share. The possibility is that it was his own personal concern. (See **Introduction** on 'Prophetic Insight'.)

The editor has described the encounter as: 'the word . . . was *by/in the hand of* the prophet Haggai'. It is a peculiarity of this document and a unique phrase describing the word coming to (or, better 'was present with') a prophet, though it is used of Moses once in Exod. 9.35. The idiom is more aligned with the prophet being an agent or messenger, generally understood to mean that Haggai was passing on what God had communicated in some manner. Repeating at 2.1, the unusual description of the mode of information in 1.3, 'by the hand of', marks the phrase as special, presumably a creation of the editor.

The prophet's name, *Haggai,* has been related to the noun *hag/hajj,* 'a feast', the term applied to the three annual pilgrimage festivals, the Feast of Weeks, of Tabernacles, and Passover. He is identified as a prophet in Ezra 5.1 and 6.14, and so identified throughout the Haggai document, but nothing more of consequence is known about him or of his role as divine messenger and bearer of promises; he stands at a distance from all other activity, almost as though he was not involved in the several crises of which he spoke. He communicated his message indirectly via questions to which others responded. Haggai then issued exaggerated promises; he appears to exempt himself from the charge of prioritizing personal housing; it was 'this people' (Hebrew *hā'ām hazzeh*) who were the problem. This format differs from many of the prophetic pronouncements that use strong condemnatory language against individuals when announcing what they claim God to have said (see Hos. 13.4-8). In referring to the community as 'this people', and the note that Yahweh was 'their God' (1.12-14), the impression is that Haggai saw himself as at a distance from the community at large, and so there is a critical tone to the phrase; it was an exclusive expression. Haggai spoke as one who was not part of *that* cohort! But, who were those he identified as 'this people'? It is clear from archaeological research that in regions beyond Jerusalem there had been only minor disruption to life for those who remained in Judaea, and a number of those returning presumably also were scattered throughout the province. Thus, only a small percentage of the population were resident in Jerusalem, so the phrase 'this people' may refer only to a small but significant number.

The role of 'governor', a functional translation of a borrowed Persian term *pḥh*, points to an administrative position deriving its authority from the appointing power to which it then reported. That governor was Zerubbabel, whose Akkadian name meant 'offspring of Babylon'. His father's name was Shealtiel who was a descendant of Jehoiachin the former king in Jerusalem taken into Babylonian exile in 587 BCE (2 Kgs 24.10-12). However, a late source (1 Chron. 3.16-19) lists him as the son of Pediah, brother of Shealtiel. Zerubbabel may have been connected intimately with the Davidic family, and, if so, then it would have been a deeply emotional matter for him and the many returning to the City of David.

Zerubbabel had been raised in a context that saw him living between two cultures—that of his Israelite forebears and that of his Babylonian neighbours. Surely there were implications in this foreign name when considering his religio-cultural views and, more generally, his identification with those who were in power in Babylon. How he, as a Jew, came to the attention of the incoming Persian administration is not known, but there is every reason to believe that Zerubbabel had formed good relations within the Babylonian administration and that this was noted by the incoming Persian authorities. He was seen as a safe pair of hands to look after Persian interests in Judaea, that he would promote Persian policies, at least to the extent that he could represent what Darius ordered for its furthest southern province and ensure that they were implemented. (See 'Haggai, Zerubbabel and Joshua' in the **Introduction**.) Unlike Haggai, Zerubbabel was a person who was able to live in two worlds and be accepted in both.

He is credited with a role in the rebuilding of the Temple in Zech. 4.9-10, while Haggai made extraordinary promises of his elevation in 2.20-23, but then nothing further is known about Zerubbabel's work as governor.

Joshua son of Jehozadak was the high priest to whom Haggai's words were also to be directed. Known by his Aramaic name, Jeshua (Ezra 2.2), he was born in Babylon and, like Zerubbabel, shaped by his life in a Jewish enclave within the cultural and religious world of Babylonia. His was also a Persian appointment, the reasons for which are not provided, the editor not being privy to this information it would seem. One can assume that the Persian authorities had come to know of him somehow and believed that, like Zerubbabel, he was open and sympathetic to their policies, compliant with Persian intensions for its distant province, while as a Jew he would satisfy local Jewish concerns for such a priestly office-bearer. About Joshua, the least known of the main players in this drama, little can be discovered as to his early career as priest. According to 2 Kgs 25.18, Joshua's grandfather Seraiah, a Levitical priest and Zadokite (1 Chron. 6.1-15), had been the chief priest in Jerusalem, was exiled to Babylon, then executed. Joshua's elevated rank within the returnee community may reflect that historical background. That he was a significant member of the new community is

Haggai 1 69

seen in that Haggai was ordered to address his words to him as one of the two community leaders. Now that there was no Judaean king, the two roles, civil and religious, were on something of an equal footing. Joshua is called high or great priest rather than chief priest as in pre-exilic times, probably indicating the higher authority of the priestly office now that there was no absolute monarch to serve as God's representative on earth. Joshua as high priest should have been expected to be the primary one to encourage Temple rebuilding as part of the renaissance of Judaean religious life, but there is no evidence of that having happened. What was it about Joshua that made him more complicit in the failure to restore the Temple and its rituals? Was he truly of the priestly line, a descendant of Zadok and Aaron through Jehozadak, as the Chronicler insists (1 Chron. 6.1-15)? Did he concede to Zerubbabel in the matter of prioritizing the people's housing? Though appointed high priest, had he been well trained, or was his religious perspective influenced and 'tainted' by the wider environment? Was he one of the conduits of Persian ideas, such as angels or 'paradise', being brought into Judaean religious language and expanding its theological vision? He certainly did not share Haggai's Deuteronomic outlook and concerns for the Temple. Being flexible about some religious matters considered non-negotiable in Deuteronomy was for Joshua not just a possibility; he clearly was open to compromise with Persia and was not one of the Judaean 'hard-liners'. Haggai and his editor clearly saw Joshua as ineffectual when it came to prioritizing the Temple renovation and motivating the people to begin the work. Even when Haggai was questioning the priests concerning torah details regarding clean and unclean matters (2.10-14), Joshua's response or advice was not sought apparently.

Throughout his report, when the editor referred to Zerubbabel and Joshua, he consistently included their patronymics and titles, presumably such detail was the particular interest of the editor for whom family descent was important. It is possible that by including the patronymics, there is an attempt to demonstrate that both Zerubbabel and Joshua had roots deep in Judah's past leadership and thus represented that past in the present context. Haggai is mostly referred to by the editor with his full identification as 'the prophet Haggai'.

1.2

This verse begins the editor's report of Haggai's mission; it uses a conventional *genre*, the messenger formula: *'Thus says the Lord of hosts'*. This introductory form can be read in two ways here: as part of messenger Haggai's speech to the two leaders; alternatively, the formula is supplied by the editor to preface Haggai's actual message, a message in which God, who appears fully aware of the community discussion regarding the Temple rebuild, quotes from that public discussion. Preference here is for the second option, given that the two formulaic phrases, *'Thus says the Lord'* and its closing form *'says the Lord'*, are *pro forma* items provided by the editor who committed the prophetic word to writing. By quoting from the community's ongoing discussion surrounding the Temple restoration programme, the editor was indicating that Haggai voiced disapproval of the decision that God's house was not for them an urgent matter. The prophet disputed the people's contention that restoring the Temple at this present time and under the present circumstances was not warranted.

There is a slight lack of clarity in 1.2 in that Haggai's message, primarily directed at the two leaders, is a criticism leveled against 'this people'. The text that follows makes it clear that the prophet's charge, while directed at both the leaders specifically, is aimed at the entire community.

Within Israelite society there had been three major leadership positions below that of the king: they were priest, prophet and sage (Jer. 18.18). Each had a defined role and assignment, and while there was a degree of agreement on many issues affecting the community, there were also occasions of dissent and clear opposition, a fact that must not be overlooked or ignored. Israel's prophets frequently looked down on sages, both local and foreign (Isa. 19.1-15; 44.25; Jer. 50.35; 51.57; Obad. 8), they criticized the priests for failing in their duties (e.g. Hos. 5.1; 6.9; Mic. 3.11), and here we have another example. By using a generalized phrase 'this people', a phrase by which the prophet exempts himself from its reference, the prophet was taunting them with a reproachful tone, marking the leaders and the whole community as questioning the importance of the Temple restoration work. It also hinted at Haggai seeing himself as above 'this people', giving reason to question how close was his relationship with the community. Was he seen as arrogant, so not of-the-people? If so, Haggai's call and its air of condescension would not have helped his cause.

What had upset Haggai, according to this editorial introduction, was the matter of priorities and the leaders' apparent failure to motivate the community to undertake the Temple repair work. That the high priest was complicit in this is remarkable. And what of the other priests who had come back in large numbers (see Ezra 1.36-53)? Surely, at least some would be sympathetic and share Haggai's concerns, but the priests and the other community members were simply labelled 'this people' and criticized for their failure to prioritize Temple repair.

When the exiles returned to Judaea/Jerusalem in 538 BCE, they, and perhaps others who had not been in exile, had more pressing things on their minds than repairing what was left of the old Temple, because for them more immediate personal needs took precedence. According to Ezra 4, there had been an early attempt under Sheshbazzar to begin reparation work, but it had been abandoned, due mainly to foreign opposition. And after all, the people had managed without a Temple and its priestly ministrations for more than 60 years, whether in Babylonian exile or in Jerusalem itself. What was so problematic with delaying Temple rebuilding? That could be taken up later when life returned to normal! Additionally, funds for the rebuilding would inevitably mean taxes to be paid, people redirected from working on their farms to take up building duties; and with harvest shortfalls menacing, Temple repair would have been seen as an extra and unwelcome burden on the community. For the moment, formal religious activity was in abeyance.

We should note that Haggai throughout uses the Deuteronomic expression 'the Lord's house'. Although the prophet's concern is for the Temple to be repaired and brought into service again, it is clear that he preferred the Deuteronomic terminology of 'house' over 'Temple'. The noun 'Temple' does not appear more than once in the entire book of Deuteronomy—its use in Deut. 23.17 is generic, not specific—while the preferred phrase throughout the full Deuteronomistic record of Joshua–2 Kings is 'the house of the Lord' (81 times). The link between Haggai and Deuteronomy seems obvious, though twice, in Hag. 2.15, 18, there is the phrase 'the Lord's Temple'. (see comments at 2.15).

The 'Lord (YHWH) of hosts' title used extensively by Haggai (and Isaiah, Jeremiah, Zechariah 8.1-8 and Malachi) points to his view of the divine one as a warrior who leads his army into battle (e.g. Isa. 1.24). Hosea (12.5) refers to Yahweh as 'the God of hosts'. The problem lies with identifying the epithet 'hosts' ($ṣ^eḇā'ôṯ$). Does it refer to the angelic crowd, the sons of God attending the enthroned God in the heavens (Gen. 32.1), to the stars and cosmic powers at his beck and call, or even to earthly agents such as were associated with the Shiloh sanctuary (1 Sam. 1.3)? The ancient cultural context allows for all of the above to inform the concept rather than defining it closely. 'Lord of hosts' connotes power and authority, and connects with the ancient Israelite notion of Yahweh's control over all things on earth and in heaven, as will be evident in 2.6-8 below.

1.3-11 Call to Rebuild the Temple

1.3 The word of the Lord was delivered by Haggai the prophet:
1.4 'Is it appropriate for you yourselves to live in your roofed houses while the house of the Lord remains in ruins?'
1.5 'Now then, this is what the Lord of hosts said:
   "Consider how you have been faring!

1.6 You have planted much seed, but brought in little,
   You eat, but are never sated,
   You drink, but are never satisfied,
   You dress, but are never warm,
   You earn money, but [put it] in a bag with holes."'
1.7 'This is what the Lord of hosts said: "Consider how you have been faring!"''
(1.8 'Go up to the mountain and fetch timber, then build the house.
   Thus I will enjoy it, and I shall be honoured', says the Lord.)
1.9 'You look for much, but behold so little!
   You brought [it] home and I snorted at it.
   Because of what? said the Lord of hosts.
   Because my house is in ruins, but you each prioritize your own home.
1.10 Therefore, the heavens above you have withheld moisture,
   The ground has failed to provide any produce.
1.11 I have demanded drought upon the land
   Upon the mountains,
   Upon the crops,
   Upon the new wine,
   Upon the oil,
   Upon the produce of the soil,
   Upon humans,
   Upon the cattle,
   And upon people's labour.'

The discourse marker 'Then the word of the Lord was delivered by Haggai, saying' begins the formal report of Haggai's speech, the message itself beginning in 1.4 with the important rhetorical question about the community's priorities—private housing or Temple repair? The two leaders—Zerubbabel, in charge of civil matters such as housing, and Joshua, in charge of religious matters—approached the issue of Temple reconstruction from their different perspectives, but both were to be criticized as failing to advance the work. The governor's priorities for private housing had popular support, while Joshua's responsibilities with regard to community religious life, if he had genuinely advocated for them, were ineffective. Both men were to be challenged by Haggai's message, Zerubbabel for his popular success and Joshua for his failure.

In 1.5, 7 the prophet challenged the whole community, calling on them to 'consider' how they have been faring recently. What had they actually achieved? The purpose of the challenge was to highlight the efforts they had made to provide for their livelihood, only to fall very short. The contrast between 'much' and 'little' is the rhetorical device illustrating the problematic situation faced, a series of natural disasters, that Haggai insists were God-induced, resulting in food shortages and a general loss of personal and financial security. The basic description of the crisis found in 1.5-6 is repeated in variant, but more explicit, form in 1.7-11. These were two versions of the prophet's challenge circulating orally and known to the editor, Haggai surely having raised the issue more than just once; so two separate versions were included by the editor. The second version, 1.7-11, is interrupted in 1.8 by a vaguely expressed order to fetch wood for the reconstruction project, and thus bring pleasure to the God who will then have a 'house' in which to dwell. It is obviously a call that belongs in some other related context but mistakenly inserted here.

1.3

This verse reports in the third person the message of Haggai, with the discourse marker taking the narrative to this next stage, that is, what Haggai actually said. The unusual idiomatic Hebrew phrase 'by the hand of Haggai' is an expression of agency—that is, by Haggai—and is found here as in v. 1, and again in 2.1. While denoting agency, there is nothing in the text that demands a revelatory source for Haggai to know of the issue, because it clearly was a current topic of community discussion that, in the words of the text, even God had heard about (1.2), and that was a matter of serious dispute.

1.4

Haggai's reported speech poses a question, already reflected in the editorial summary statement in 1.2. The rhetorical question, 'Is it the time for you yourselves to *occupy* (your) paneled houses?' (NRSV), is challenging and accusatory, expecting a negative answer from the audience. The use of the independent Hebrew pronoun 'you', as in the NRSV 'you yourselves', emphasizes the point. Haggai refuses to accept the view that private dwellings should have priority over the Lord's house. He was incensed that the community did not see Temple repair as a priority at the time, especially as it had lain as an untended ruin for more than 60 years. Their failure to prioritize rebuilding the Lord's house implied so much for Haggai—disrespect for their God and the covenant he initiated, demeaning their role as God's chosen people, failing to keep torah, the Law's demands, and failing to honour God. Those returned from Babylon in 538 BCE, or soon after, had spent the intervening 18 or so years working to re-establish normal life from amid the ruins. This would have been Zerubbabel's area of concern, civil affairs. Clearly, religious ritual concerns, which should have been Joshua's focus, were further down the list of necessary works; and Joshua's presence, along with that of the returning priests, had had little impact on changing the priorities that were set. There is no reference to him initiating or encouraging the repair effort, nor of organizing the practicalities to get the building work done.

While the basic meaning of the Hebrew term $s^ep\hat{u}n\hat{i}m$, literally 'coverings', used to describe the houses of 'this people' is clear, its application here is apparently not. In 1 Kgs 6.9, 15 the root *spn* is applied to descriptions of the ceiling or roof of Solomon's Temple, and they are specified as cedar panels or decorations. That is not so specified here, and the whole context is more general. Suggestions that the people's homes decorated with cedar panels implies expensive homes and selfish values are unreasonable and unfounded. The 'coverings' almost certainly are roof coverings. Furthermore, the prophet's complaint relates to 'this people', that is, the whole community, so the contrast the editor has made between the people's homes and the Temple site is not one of elegant, cedar-paneled walls over against a devastated Temple site, because such disparity would apply to only a small number of houses, namely the homes of the community leaders or the wealthy. Many, perhaps the majority, of the residents of Jerusalem and the wider province would be living in tents or in very modest dwellings and not in substantial and fine cedar-lined homes. The prophet's criticism would not apply so widely unless he was deliberately exaggerating for effect. And what of Haggai's own house? What was he living in? Something nicely finished and furnished, or . . . ? The Temple site had been devastated by fire, meaning all the major timbers supporting the roof had been burned, leaving the site open to the weather. Here Haggai's complaint was that 'this people' all have a roof over their heads while the Lord's house is completely open to the elements. Whether his description is hyperbole or not, it is a situation he finds unacceptable.

At a more mundane level, repair work on the Temple would inevitably take many people away from working their fields and from other subsistence demands where their labour was sorely needed. Such a building project would be a serious impost on the people in terms of time and taxes, and especially so when life was uncertain and harvests meagre. There were good reasons for the general reluctance to pursue Temple rebuilding: taxes would need to be levied for a large construction project as money offered by Persia would not have been adequate for a long Temple-building process, and taxes still had to be paid to Persia. Haggai's subsequent promise of treasures flowing in from the nations, a seemingly impossible dream, would not move many to take up the building challenge when faced by more immediate personal and family needs.

There is a play on words around the use of 'house' and, more importantly from an editorial view, an echo of the encounter between Nathan the prophet and David in 2 Samuel 7. There, David was enthusiastic about building a 'house' for Yahweh but was thwarted by Nathan's promise that God would build a 'house' for David. Here the prophet's enthusiasm, like that of David, was for the 'house' to be built by the community for God's glory and enjoyment.

The text suggests that there had been wide destruction of the Temple building and its fittings when the Babylonians invaded in 587 BCE, but that the 'bones' of the building were still there. Almost certainly, some of the remaining stonework would have been 'stolen' in order to repair some of the houses and buildings in the city during the intervening years. Haggai's position was that what remained of the Temple was not currently adequate for the necessary religious rituals, though Ezra 3 speaks of the leaders and priests setting out to build the Temple altar on which they then offered burnt offerings, linking it with keeping the Feast of Booths, a harvest festival, followed by an almost regular round of Temple activity. If Ezra's report is to be dated around 458 BCE then there is a question as to accuracy with regard to Temple activity in Haggai's time. The important thing to note is the reluctance or inability of Joshua the religious leader to change the broader community decision about priorities.

1.5-6 'Consider . . .' I

An initial discourse marker 'But now' follows the rhetorical question with another challenge introduced by the messenger formula *'Thus says the Lord'* (see also v. 7). It is addressed to 'you' plural, so one asks: Who is included in this reference? It certainly includes the two leaders but may be of wider embrace. The call is for 'you' to reflect on the situation in the community at large. In order to encourage the people to begin working on Temple restoration, Haggai suggested people take a hard look at the current reality they were all enduring and to reflect on what he regarded as its implications. In the prophet's mind there was a direct connection between the current difficulties being experienced and the failure to rebuild the Temple; the people saw no such connection.

'Consider how you have fared', literally 'put your heart on (think about) your ways (pl.)!' is the first use of the set phrase, an idiom repeated in 1.7. The phrase 'put you heart/mind upon' is one of a variety of similar expressions relating to knowing or acknowledging something, to take matters seriously. In this case, what had to be thought through was described as 'your ways' or 'your pathways', which includes, among other things, a manner of living, or here, read broadly as 'your circumstances', 'what has happened to you'. It can be read negatively as well; so here it could be yet another way of speaking about the decision not to proceed with Temple repair. The wide semantic range of the noun *derek*, 'way, road, path', carries both active and passive senses—the way one operates or lives, and what happens to one on the journey. Even the journey to death is described as the 'way of all humanity' (1 Kgs 2.2) and a woman's monthly cycle as the 'way of women' (Gen. 31.35).

The content of 'your ways' is then specified in v. 6 as a shortage of basic needs—a shortage of food, wine, clothing and employment. These were the current circumstances, the way things were. What it signified in Haggai's mind was to be explained in 1.10-11, in the expanded second call to 'consider'.

1.6

Using contrast, 'much' and 'little', a series of three negative phrases each introduced by the negating 'but there is no . . .', and two examples of lack—no warm clothing (heading into winter!) and poor wages. Haggai paints a harsh picture of the present reality, a reality that presumably would have affected the two leaders just as much as every other member of the community, including Haggai himself. Under this presentation every member of that community, including innocent children and animals, were all charged with refusing to complete Temple repairs. How long was it before the prophet thought to link the material shortages with God's intervention? Did he not think of it until the day that God spoke to him, or had he been wondering for some time how best to understand and explain the daily crisis the community faced? How empathetic was he? Despite their best efforts to provide for their most basic needs, the whole community was suffering shortages in all areas. No matter how much seed they planted, the harvest was inadequate; food and drink were in short supply; furthermore, there was a lack of warm clothing, and those who were daily workers found that their meagre wages were insufficient to support themselves and their families—'you earn money, but [put it] in a bag with holes'. The direct impact of these shortages affected every member of the community, the three leaders included. The language attributed to Haggai in painting this picture appears drawn from his theological source document, Deuteronomy; Deut. 28.38 uses these exact same contrasts: 'you shall carry *much* seed into the field but shall gather *little* in'.

It is important to remember that the kind of situation pictured was not something new in 520 BCE; drought and limited harvests in the region were regular experiences due to Judaea's geographical location in the mountains that ran north to south along its spine, to its poor soils, to devastating hot winds in summer, and a climate of restricted and unpredictable rainfall; Judaea was a backwater in every sense of the word. While Judaea's northern border area and western slopes had a better climate and soils, the further south one moves the more difficult conditions become, until meeting the southern desert. Judaea's history was dogged with an ever-present threat of drought and famine—see Gen. 12.10; 26.1; 42.1–43.2; 1 Kgs 18.1. From this standpoint, the people would have seen nothing particularly unusual in their present difficulties, for that was a frequent reality in this location—until Haggai offered his explanation, hoping to enlighten them.

The two versions of the people's difficulties in 1.6 and 1.7-9, 'Consider . . .' I and 'Consider . . .' II, lead into Haggai's explanation in 1.10-11. It was Haggai's Deuteronomic ideology that convinced him that there was a direct link between this present harvest crisis—one that was probably no worse than any other—and targeted divine action (Deut. 7.12-16). It was an explanation that, if accepted, meant that Judaea was doomed to an eternity of God-induced harvest failures, as had happened throughout its past! To link this reality to national disobedience was an ideologically based conclusion.

1.7-11 'Consider . . .' II

This section offers a second version of the initial call to 'consider' in 1.5-6. It too is built around the theme of 'much/little' and the God-induced shortfall in the current harvest, along with its impact on both humans and animals.

Intruding inexplicably into this version of the call is 1.8, which turns momentarily to the subject of fetching timber for the Temple building. It is an independent memory misplaced by the editor.

1.7

Again, Haggai, using the imperative voice as a divine messenger, calls on the returnees and others to consider the harsh realities of everyday life. The repetition of 1.5 here may be viewed in two ways: (1) as a literary inclusion that then brackets 1.5-7 and intended for emphasis, or (2) as the introduction to a second call to 'consider' that takes up the same theme of 'much/little' noted in 1.5-6. It has been traditional to view 1.7 as an inclusion rounding out the initial call. However, recognizing how oral traditions develop from multiple presentations that then circulate simultaneously within a community as slightly differing versions, we see that the structure and common theme of 1.5-6 and 1.7-11 point more convincingly to them being two versions of the same call. Here, the preference is for 1.7 to be seen as beginning a second version of the call to 'consider' in 1.5-6. The editor who compiled this report had access to variant versions of the prophet's oral message; he was aware that the remembered words of Haggai circulating in the community were not always identical, due to Haggai presenting his concerns in different settings or because popular chatter as the message was shared had made for slightly differing but basically similar accounts. Formal and linguistic features remained the same while details could vary. The editor has included two versions without attempting to co-ordinate or smooth out any minor discrepancies. The same editorial issue will be argued to apply to the case of 2.15-17 and 2.18-19 below. (One can also compare the accounts in Genesis 12, 20 and 26 in which the ancestress—Sarah or Rebekah?—is taken by the pharaoh or Abimelech as other examples of how stories 'travel' within an oral culture.)

1.8

Verse 8 bears all the hallmarks of being completely out of place, intruding between the call to 'consider' in 1.7 that continues in v. 9 as the past/present situation was again addressed. Some argue that this unusual intrusion means that v. 8 is being highlighted. While 1.8 may say something important about the divine intent for the Lord's house, it is totally irrelevant to the call to reflect on the food shortage and is best seen as an extraneous element, something Haggai may have said on some other occasion relating to the Temple's purpose; it must be considered separately from 1.7, 9-11.

The command in 1.8 is for the people to climb the mountain and collect timber with which to repair the 'house'. If the mountain referred to is the Temple mount, none would find timber there! Perhaps 'mountain' is used as a collective; so the command may have been for people to head for the hills, the last place where suitable timber was to be found in that part of the central mountains. Such a call simply highlights further the anomaly of v. 8 at this location. As noted, the command itself has nothing to do with the call to reflect on their difficult situation, nor have they as yet responded to Haggai and demonstrated a readiness to reprioritize their work in favour of the Temple. The verse is clearly misplaced, and this view is further strengthened when noting that the concluding element of the two-part messenger form, *'says the Lord'*, is inserted to mark its close (see further Appendix A).

As the text stands, 1.8 is a simple order to fetch timber for repairing the Temple. This order is so out of place that it is difficult, if not impossible, to know where it might fit in the overall narrative. Certainly, the matter of timber supply relates to what was especially lacking for the Temple repair. Stonework would have been damaged by fire in the Babylonian sacking of the Temple, and some of what remained would have been 'stolen' by residents to build or repair their own homes, but the woodwork and soft material components would have disappeared in the conflagration. Timber would need to be found to finish the Temple, but little would be available locally, and especially not in the hill country due to poor and shallow soils unsuitable for growing timber. Perhaps in the valleys to the north and west there might have been some smaller trees available, but not the large trees required for roof trusses and the like. Logistics for the Temple rebuild does not appear to have been a concern expressed by Haggai other than in this isolated and errant verse.

When Solomon planned to build the first Temple, he contracted with King Hiram for the supply of Lebanese cedar (1 Kgs 5), there being no suitable timber resources locally in Judah for a large building whose wide spaces required spanning. Buildings in the region were generally of stone, of which there was an abundance, while Jerusalem's environs did not support the growth of large trees suitable for roofing support in such a building project. It is not possible to clarify what Haggai's commands in the present context expect, other than ordering people to go fetch timber.

What is interesting is that the order to fetch timber is clearly presented as being Yahweh's own demand, and related to the desire to 'let me take pleasure in it' (a restored Temple) and 'let me be honoured' or 'glorify myself'. These words, if nothing else, do give an insight into the document's theology; God's priority, according to Yahweh's messenger, is a building suitable for the divine one to feel pleased, a place of prestige where Yahweh can receive public acknowledgment, be honoured or worshipped. Regardless of whether the Hebrew passive verb forms used have cohortative or reflexive nuance, the order, as a word from God, suggests that the Temple was to assume priority over the needs of the people. Does it mean that Haggai saw God's desire for his personal pleasure as more important than the people's livelihood? There is something troubling about what this demand seems to require if understood literally, though it does reflect a theology perhaps consistent with a priestly mindset, a demand for obeisance before the powerful 'Lord of hosts'. It also intimates a widespread belief that a beautiful sacred space is required in which the national God may dwell.

The final phrase, *'says the Lord'*, is the concluding element in the messenger form, surely out of place if the verse is integral to the section 1.7-11. It is clear that the verse is misplaced.

1.9

The call to 'consider' begun in v. 7 now resumes after the interruption of v. 8. Repetition of the 'much/little' contrast in what is a second version of 1.6 expands the reference to the people's expectations upon their return from exile. The initial Hebrew verb *pnh*, indicates a turning, whether toward or away from an object, and can also suggest turning to look at or look for something, moving in a new direction. The latter seems to catch the sense, so the initial half-verse speaks generally of high expectations that were not realized. Because the statement is very general, the need is to identify what 'little' was achieved; the list provided in 1.6 must be seen to apply here as well, namely crops, wine, clothing and wages. The problem the community faced was even greater in this second version, since whatever was achieved was then dismissed by God as insignificant. The rendering 'brought it home' does not define the 'it', but it must surely refer to the same farm products as listed in 1.6, and especially so if 1.7, 9 is a second version of 1.5-6, as is being argued. Surprisingly, perhaps, the prophet then advises the listeners that even the little that had resulted from their labour, Yahweh 'blew it away' (1.9a).

Haggai, on behalf of God, says literally, 'I snorted at it', the verb expressing contempt for an action (see also Mal. 1.13). Such a characterization of the divine one was far from good news, scoffing at or belittling the people's attempts to achieve their goal of self-sufficiency. However, there is very little significant difference between this harsh way of speaking of divine intervention and the form used in 1.11; in both cases the prophet concluded that God was the one deliberately frustrating the people's attempt to sustain themselves. What Haggai did then in 1.9b-10a is to explain the reason behind what he believed was divine intervention.

In order to minimize the problem many see inherent in Haggai's theological explanation of a divine attitude imposing hardship, some commentators have offered alternative suggestions: that vermin ate much of the harvest; that something unusual but unnamed happened to reduce the volume and value of the harvest; that the grain lost its nutritional value. All such are vain attempts to circumvent the obvious fact that, according to the text as it now stands, God intervened and decimated the expected harvests, together with causing other associated difficulties for both humans and animals. Is this a case of the prophet's distorted theology or ideology, or was it a natural outcome of the Deuteronomic agenda preferred by Haggai?

Verses 9c and 9d both begin with a Hebrew preposition that assigns cause or reason—so 'because of what?' or 'why?' the Lord asks. Why did God 'snort' in contempt at their attempts to succeed agriculturally? While God's house lies in ruins, Haggai charges the people with literally 'running each to his (own) house', a figurative expression that is thought to express giving priority or preferences to one's own housing concerns. The notion of God 'snorting' in his anger and disgust at their prioritizing of domestic needs over that of restoring his Temple can only be understood against the background of the prophet's commitment to the Deuteronomic ideology, an unshakeable belief that God, via a weaponizing of natural climatic changes such as drought, deliberately intervened in the human programme to achieve his own purposes. It was a theology that accepted the notion of the Lord of hosts' unbridled power, but one lacking all compassion and humanity. It is coordinated with the verb 'strike' in 2.17 describing the divine action in even more stark terms.

What needs to be considered here also is how Haggai seems not to be concerned by the irony in his argument. The same Yahweh who had sent enemy forces to destroy Judah and the Temple in 587 BCE as an act of punishment for years of provocation by its kings, and by Manasseh in particular (2 Kgs 24.2-4, 13), was ultimately responsible for the Temple situation being as it now was—the devastated building currently lying abandoned. The DH editors had accounted for its destruction in terms of divine intervention: God, in fact, was directly responsible for the Temple lying in ruins in 520 BCE. Now, however, according to the prophet, God wanted it rebuilt without delay. (See 'Theological Ideas' in the **Introduction**.)

1.10

Haggai's justification for God's anger and contempt are here spelled out— and spelled out in terms of the theological principle seen most clearly in the book of Deuteronomy. The initial 'therefore' transitions to the justification for action in treating the people so harshly. Haggai the messenger explains that it is the heavens and the earth together who have acted against the people; both have conspired to ensure that the harvest failed. These climatic conditions are, according to this view, physical evidence of divine disfavour (see Deut. 28.1-12), a curse. The natural world itself, in league with God, is charged with having brought about the people's suffering. The natural crises experienced, however, were common in the Judaean region, as already noted, so unless the issue here is some *extraordinary* drought and harvest failure requiring an *extraordinary* explanation, there would be no particular reason to attribute this one crisis to a specific divine curse. Furthermore, Haggai's Deuteronomic evaluation regarded the stalled Temple project as an act of deliberate disobedience rather than it being merely a communal decision to delay the work; the delay was not sin, nor was it disobedience. Nature's fickle climatic variations were interpreted as divine disfavour with 'this people'.

1.11

Using a play on the Hebrew root word *ḥrb*—rendered in NRSV as 'desolation in 1.4, 9 and 'drought' in 1.11—the text links the Temple's sad condition intimately with that of the people and even of their animals, which are equally 'punished' during this God-induced drought. It is an itemized expansion on the divine action noted in 1.10, reflecting Haggai's belief that God used natural phenomena as a means of punishing frail humanity and the creatures under their care. It is not that the people had committed some grave sin, as some want to assume, for nowhere in this brief document is the word mentioned, a point often overlooked, nor is there any serious accusation leveled against the people other than their priority, a choice to which Haggai objects.

The editor in v. 10 personalized the heavens and the earth as themselves deciding to withhold moisture and decimate the land's produce; they both are the actor subjects. In v. 11 God was identified more directly as calling for a drought, suggesting that a third party, nature itself, was being summoned to carry out the divine plan. Both verses use a very indirect form of reporting. The current crisis, however, in Haggai's mind remains as the outworking of planned destructive activity by Haggai's God.

According to Deut. 7.12-16; 11.14 etc., the grain, new wine, oil, and other agricultural products represent material blessings, and, as blessings, their supply was dependent on the community being faithful to Yahweh, who gave the land. Haggai argues from effect to cause, so understands the people's delay in Temple repair as unfaithfulness despite never justifying or explaining his judgment in so many words. Whether at some point Haggai spoke more about why the community was deserving of the divine curse as outlined in Deut. 28.16-19 is not discernible from the text that remains.

1.12-15a The People Respond

1.12 Then Zerubbabel son of Shealtiel and Joshua son of Jehozadak the high priest, with all the rest of the people, responded to the voice of the Lord their God and to the message of the prophet Haggai whom the Lord their God had sent;
the people were in awe of the Lord's presence.
1.13 Then Haggai, the messenger of the Lord, conveyed the Lord's message to the people: 'I am with you', says the Lord.
1.14 Then the Lord inspired Zerubbabel son of Shelatiel, governor of Judaea, Joshua son of Jehozadak, the high priest, and all the rest of the people so that they (all) came and worked on the house of the Lord of hosts who was their God.
1.15 On the twenty-fourth day of the sixth month in the second year of Darius.

Here the editor reports how the people responded to the prophet's challenge to begin the rebuilding work; in summary, they all, Zerubbabel, Joshua and the 'rest of the people', are said to have responded positively to the call. Haggai had challenged the community's decision about what was most important to it, namely housing and livelihood. He argued that the current troubles were God-induced. Surely, that was not a comforting message to hear. Nevertheless, that explanation is here said to have been heard and acted upon by all (1.12) as a community-wide response, though one suspects that there is an element of hyperbole in that description. Any suggestion that the community 'obeyed' (NRSV) God's call in Haggai's words is misleading, for the message was never a demand for obedience; yes, they did respond positively according to the report, the nature of the response being that some, a 'remnant' of the *ʿām* (people), began to offer themselves for Temple reconstruction duty (1.14). Haggai assured those volunteers that God was present among them, a crucial reminder in view of what had transpired over the past 60 years of humiliation at the hands of enemies. It was an assurance, repeated in 2.4, linked with the Exodus tradition (Exod. 32–34) that gave tribal Israel its identity. Here, the prophet recalled that foundation tradition, hoping that it would resound in people's minds. Yet those words of assurance meant nothing without some outward manifestation. It was said to have manifested itself in God 'stirring up the spirit' of all participants, leaders and people as one, and work on the Temple was begun—slowly.

Three times in this section, and this section only, the editor has used the impersonal third-person reference, 'the Lord their God' when referring to the community's relationship with Yahweh, although there is some small doubt about the use in v. 12b in view of the LXX reading 'to them' (*ʾelēhem*) in lieu of 'God' (*ʾelōhîm*). One can presume that there is some intention in this feature, namely a covenantal emphasis; the editorial note, however, does put the prophet at some distance from his audience, similar to his referring to the community as 'this people' (1.2).

1.12

It is Zerubbabel and Joshua together with that cohort described as 'all the remnant of the people' who are said to have 'listened and responded positively' (the Hebrew verb *šāmaʿ* embraces both components into one concept—to narrow it to 'obey' is very limiting) to what Haggai had said. Given that the prophet's message is initially directed specifically to the leadership (1.1), it is clear from their response here that the two officials each had been complicit in the community reluctance to prioritize the Temple over personal housing.

The phrase 'the rest of the people', sometimes rendered as 'remnant', implies that not everybody joined in the work, but it is unclear whom the phrase does include. The phrase is used three times in the report (1.12, 14;

2.2) and could refer to the small population of Jerusalem, excluding those who were scattered throughout Judaea's towns and villages; it may relate to those who chose to return from Babylonian exile; it could also be those who remained behind after the so-called elite had been removed to Babylon. What it does include is that small portion of the population who were convinced by Haggai's appeal and who were physically able to participate in building work. There is not sufficient evidence to determine more specifically the cohort to which this phrase refers. In true hyperbolic style, the editor insists that 'all', including the governor and high priest, are said to have responded positively to 'the voice of the Lord', which is 'the words of the prophet Haggai'—a hendiadys expressing the notion of a unity of mind between the prophet and his God. (See 'Prophetic Insight' in the **Introduction.**)

The editor notes that following Haggai's message all three elements 'responded' (Hebrew *šāma'*) to Haggai's call. The response echoes the frequent use of this keyword in Deuteronomy (e.g. Deut. 28.1, 2, 13, 15), where positively responding to divine command is required in order to obtain or retain the promised blessings. In parallel with this, the editor notes that the people 'feared' Yahweh. This common rendering in English is completely inadequate as the Hebrew root word has a semantic range that extends from a positive attitude of awe and wonder with respect to the divine, to a healthy dread of potential negative outcomes.

Twice in this verse the phrase 'the Lord their God' appears. While Haggai prefers to use the title 'Lord of hosts' to refer to God, here the notion of the Lord in the role of the national deity is emphasized.

1.13

Haggai is here characterized as God's 'messenger' rather than as prophet. Whether there is some subtle change in emphasis intended in presenting his role as divine spokesman or not, one feature is clear: there is a literary play as the messenger (Hebrew *mal'āk*) delivers his message (Hebrew *mal'ākût*), and as a result the community commences work (Hebrew *m^elā'kāh*) on the 'house of the Lord' (1.14).

As God's spokesman or messenger, Haggai's presence in the community is a constant reminder of God's presence as well, assuring the people that Yahweh will be with them as they undertake the project; he is/will be present. What this presence entailed is not defined, but 'I (am) with you' (Hebrew *'^anî 'itt^ekem*) is a phrase inextricably related to the covenantal relationship between Yahweh and his people (see also 2.4). The statement recalls Moses's encounter with God as pictured in Exod. 3.14; 6.2-3 where God revealed his identity as 'I am who I am' (*'ehyeh '^ašer 'ehyeh*). The

Hebrew verb *hyh* used there suggests a presence, a 'being with' (see also Isa. 41.10; 43.5; Amos 5.14). In contrast to their sense of God's absence during their exile, this promise may have been the catalyst for a renewed sense of their covenant relationship. That divine presence was not something abstract, or a warm feeling; it was expressed in practical terms in the activity of the 'spirit' that followed.

1.14

The positive response from at least some in the community was accompanied by divine action, 'stirring up' the spirits (or hearts) of both leaders and the people who then came together to work on the Temple. It is interesting that throughout the narrative Haggai is presented by the editor as playing no role other than as questioner and promise maker; he is a distant figure, not one of 'this people', so the housing issue does not seem to apply to him—what did he live in?—nor does he participate in any Temple reconstruction. Did he see himself as above manual work? More importantly, there is lacking any mention of the basic needs in the building programme such as a person(s) to supervise the work, the labour supply and material logistics, unless 1.8 and the mysterious demand for timber hints at information not included in the editor's report. It is as though Haggai had no interest in personally organizing to have the Temple rebuilt. How did he see the work being done? From where would he source the necessary timber? Haggai's role was to criticize the people for not advancing the rebuild, but the report is silent as to how that might be achieved, especially under the current crisis.

Verse 14 is built around a threefold repetition involving the word 'spirit' as Zerubbabel, Joshua and the small working community it seems (apart from Haggai) were 'stirred up' to participate in the rebuilding (Ezra 1.5). 'Stir up', a verb describing one waking from sleep, is a verb frequently used to recount events and actions as having been prompted by an external divine power, an idiom for God at work in and through a variety of individuals. In Isa. 41.2 it is applied to Cyrus, God's 'messiah', who then released the exiles from Babylonian captivity, enabling them to return to Jerusalem. Jeremiah uses the imagery also (Jer. 51.1, 11); see also Ezra 1.5. To understand the meaning of 'spirit' here, we turn to the account of the building of the movable Tent of Meeting in Exod. 35.10–36.2. While the Hebrew noun *rûaḥ* has a wide semantic range (wind, breath, spirit), it also has a particular application to one's practical skill, regarding that skill, whether natural or learned, as a divine gift. In this view, whatever accomplishments a person demonstrates, they can be attributed not just to the person's innate skill or training but to something derived from the beneficence of one's God or gods. Just as God is said to 'stir up' the men and women who constructed and beautified the Tent (Exod. 35.31), so here the editor regards the range of practical abilities necessary for restoring the Temple as God-given; each was inspired to contribute their skills as the task required.

The phrase 'the house of the Lord of hosts, their God', identifies the Temple as the dwelling place of God among his people.

1.15a

According to the editor's record, the restoration work was begun 24 days after Haggai is said to have received the message from God, that is, September 21, 520 BCE. It is pointless to speculate about what was going on between the day Haggai is said to have received a word from God and the beginning of Temple restoration work, but it does allow for a period of negotiation by Haggai with members of the community with regard to beginning that work. As noted above, there are no details available regarding responsibility for supervision or logistics and other arrangements for the building work to progress. The importance of putting into the record a starting date for building, whether historically accurate or not, notes that the prophet's challenge to the community was at last effective. The date here implies that the work was begun on that day, but with no indication in the rest of the document as to how the work was supplied and progressed, who might have been in charge if it wasn't Joshua, or when the work was actually finished. This latter means that the editor's report was largely confined to circumstances leading only to getting the rebuilding work started. Neither in Haggai nor in Zechariah is there any reference to the Temple's progress or completion. It is only from the account in Ezra 6.14-15 that we know of the Temple's completion in 516–515 BCE.

The presence of another date here is in the nature of a literary inclusion that rounds out the editor's First Dated Message (1.1-15a).

Haggai 2

1.15b—2.9 Second Dated Message

1.15b In the second year of King Darius,
2.1 on the twenty-first day of the seventh month, the word of the Lord came by the prophet Haggai:
2.2 '[Haggai] Speak now to Zerubbabel son of Shealtiel, the governor of Judea, and to Joshua son of Jehozadak, the high priest, and to the rest of the people and ask:
2.3 "Who among you who remain have seen this house in its former glory? What do you see when looking at it now? Is it not like nothing in your eyes?
2.4 Now, have courage, Zerubbabel! *says the Lord*; "Have courage Joshua, son of Jehozadak, high priest! Have courage all people of the land! *says the Lord*; Work! For I am with you, *says the Lord of hosts*."
2.5 ... the word that I covenanted with you when you departed Egypt. My spirit stands among you; do not fear!'
2.6 For this is what the Lord of hosts says: 'Yet again in a little [while] I am about to shake the heavens and the earth, the sea and the dry land,
2.7 I will cause all the nations to shudder, and the valuable things from all the foreign nations will come, and I will fill this house with glory, *says the Lord of hosts*.
2.8 Mine is the silver, and mine is the gold, *says the Lord of hosts*.
2.9 The final glory of this house will be more than that of the first, *says the Lord of hosts*.'

The editor described Haggai's visit to the Temple restoration team, listing the rhetorical questions he put to them, along with the promises he made, assuring them that the final result of their labour would be a splendid Temple accompanied by a return of *shalom*, 'peace/well-being'. The language of the report clearly implies that the series of three questions to be put to the community (2.3) derive from God, as do the three words of challenge ('take courage'), the imperative to keep working, and assurance of divine presence (2.4). One can wonder whether it was God who decided what questions Haggai needed to ask the priests since the question-format is integral to the way in which the editor presented the prophet's every encounter with his audience. The questions were a rhetorical device central to the editor's presentation, and the answers here were obvious before the asking. (See 'Prophetic Insights' in the **Introduction**.)

The message, dated to seven weeks after the first, that is, October 17, 520 BCE, opens with a note about Haggai addressing the two leaders as well as 'the remnant of the people' in 1.15b–2.2, making it clear that his major concern is still the failure of the two leaders who were responsible for the community's overall welfare and for the delay in Temple repair. The impression given is that Haggai called a meeting of the whole community at the site of the ruined Temple to scold them, though it does not preclude individual meetings separately with Zerubbabel and with Joshua, and then further meetings with the workers on site. There is no mention of Joshua, or any priests, or any supervisor being in command of the workers and overseeing the work. After several weeks working on site there probably would have been some progress visible, such as clearing the rubble and beginning to gather resources, but the level of obvious progress in those opening weeks would have been minimal. Hence, when Haggai came to inspect the work, he was unreasonably concerned at its slow pace and its apparent deficiencies.

As was his wont, the editor, presenting Haggai's interaction with his audience throughout primarily as questions (see 1.4, 9; 2.12, 16, 19), asked three things of them regarding the quality of the work thus far done. The rhetorical questions anticipate negative responses and reveal Haggai's (and God's?) deep disappointment with what he was seeing. However, though said to be stirred by the 'spirit' when the work was begun (1.14), the group of workers, who were probably at best semi-skilled and with limited resources in comparison with what had been available to Solomon, had eventually shown willingness to begin the task. The very disparaging or hectoring tone of the questions apparently did not discourage them. The prophet then pivoted to a more pastoral role and called for all to 'take courage', to find strength in a promise that Yahweh was present (2.4), a promise noted also in the comforting words in 1.13 (see note).

It is conceivable that the editor has drawn on the tradition that an earlier Joshua was called to 'be courageous' following his elevation to community leadership after the demise of Moses (Josh. 1.6-7). The intertextual connection would also explain the poignant reference to the Exodus tradition in 2.5. That traditional story had been on the lips of every Israelite at festivals and home celebrations for centuries—leaving a foreign 'prison' for the promised land. Now, it had happened again; the 'people of the land' had been led home from exile and the divine presence was again being assured.

All that was needed now was for this Joshua the high priest to fulfil his priestly responsibility.

Continuing his concern for a glorious Temple, Haggai promised that God would 'shake' the entire cosmos and the surrounding nations to provide the gold and silver, the treasures, to put the finishing touches on the Temple and treasury ensuring that it was a magnificent building. Not only did the prophet envision a glorious Temple, he saw it as eventually exceeding the wonder of Solomon's Temple. A cosmic shake-up demonstrating the power held by the Lord of hosts has little relevance to the building project *per se*, but to 'shake all the nations' was a claim for God's power and control of the international world and especially his power over the enemies. God would shake loose the treasures they held and see them flow into Jerusalem for the glorification of the Temple project. This bold claim by Haggai came against the background of the grave doubts about God's power felt by the people of Judah when overrun by the Babylonians in 587 BCE, bringing about Jerusalem's and the Temple's destruction and the loss of its treasures. Despite the excessive hyperbole, these promises elicited a positive response in the workers. Haggai also promised a future of *shalom*, peace, security and well-being.

1.15b–2.1 Second Message: October 17, 520 BCE

The Glory of the Restored Temple Assured
The date given is the twenty-first day of the seventh month in the second year of Darius's reign, 520 BCE, roughly a month and a half after the restoration work is said to have begun (1.15a). The date is October 17, apparently coinciding with the final day of the Feast of Booths, the great celebration in the fields at the end of the annual harvest. Whether that year there was much to celebrate, given the harvest shortfall, is questionable. It is the editor who has supplied this date, using exactly the same form of wording as in the first case (1.1). Perhaps the editor has accurately recorded the prophet's daily schedule, but it is also possible that he has developed one as the literary structure around which to hang his narrative. In any event, seeking some significance in God's timing of the second message proves elusive. Why on this day and not another, especially as the work had barely progressed by then?

There is a slight textual question here in that the 'word of the Lord' is said to have come *by means of* Haggai (*bᵉyad-haggay*), as in 1.1, with the command being that Haggai should himself ask a series of questions. He is both the vehicle and the object of this message, an imperative, 'Speak now', calling for him to address his audience. The anomaly came about presumably because the editor has simply used his *pro forma* wording. Some commentators, however, suggest that the Hebrew *bᵉyad-haggay* actually means 'to Haggai', a very convenient attempt to remove the syntax problem. That problem was apparently realized by later scroll copyists as the version of Haggai found in the Murabbaʻat caves in 1952 had changed 'by the hand of' to 'to' Haggai.

2.2-3

Haggai is commanded again to address all parties, Zerubbabel and Joshua as the community leaders, and those described as 'the remnant of the people' (see 1.12, 14), presumably a reference to those who had changed their priorities, who may have completed their own housing construction, and any who were free for whatever reason to join the Temple builders, such as a bevy of day labourers. It does not seem to include a community-wide audience.

The first question Haggai puts is literally: '*Who* among you (pl.), the surviving one(s), have seen this house in its former glory?' If a rhetorical question, then it affirms that none present had seen the original Temple. If it was a genuine question, it may imply that there have been some present who, whether left behind in Jerusalem in 587 or now returning from exile, were at least 80 years old and able to readily recall having seen the fabulous Temple before it was devastated in 587 BCE. The possibility that there were folk who had seen the original Temple is remote, given the average life span of people of that time, and also the reality that any who could remember the Solomonic Temple would have only the vaguest of childhood memories. In any event, none could foretell how the present ruin would eventually look by comparison with the former building. The 'former glory' in this context may refer to the former Temple's architectural grandeur or spectacle rather than the divine presence that was said to occupy it.

A second question challenges the audience to consider the reputation of the glorious old Temple with what they see lying in ruins around them, and asks: '*What* do you see now?' The question really answers itself; it is rhetorical, a challenge, rather than seeking information, for what they had achieved thus far was minimal, and the outlook far from glorious.

This leads into a third rhetorical question: '*Is it not* like nothing in your eyes?' Even if Haggai was a younger person who had actually seen the earlier Temple, his question implied that the people would agree with him that their building effort to date had produced nothing to compare with the reported marvel that was the old Solomonic Temple. It is clear that the prophet was drawing a sharp contrast between the reputed magnificence of Solomon's Temple and what now stood in its place. There was always the possibility that comparing what stood before them on the old Temple site with what they imagined Solomon's Temple to have been would be so disappointing that they would give up. Haggai's intent was to drive the project forward, and, according to the text, the challenge he put before them in these questions did have that positive effect.

As noted above, the text of this verse states that the questions Haggai was to ask were supplied by God. One can so regard them, or alternatively view the questions as the editor's way of describing Haggai's approach to the audience. In either case, readers are presented with a carefully constructed narrative consisting of three rhetorical questions, three calls to be courageous, and concluding with a command to continue the work, grounded in the assurance of the divine presence (2.4).

2.4

Haggai calls on Zerubbabel, Joshua and 'all people of the land', the same three parties as in 1.12, to 'be strong', encouraging all with the promise 'I am with you, says the Lord of hosts'. Throughout the text of Haggai there are several phrases used that identify his wider group of addressees: 'the people', 'all the remnant of the people', 'this people', 'this nation', and here 'all the people of the land'. It is conceivable that the latter is intending to embrace every individual in Judaea, whereas the former may indicate specific groups of varying sizes and identity within the community. It is uncertain whether the editor intends this kind of distinction, and, if so, on what basis distinctions can be realistically made.

The encouragement to continue their repair work is predicated on the formal promise of a divine presence that was meant to encourage the workers, the prophet announcing the divine imprimatur on the work they were undertaking. It was an assurance that the covenant relationship, once strained by their defeat by the Babylonians and the subsequent exile, was now a thing of the past—God was still with them.

The tradition of Joshua, the servant of Moses, being encouraged to 'be strong' as he took over the leadership of God's people (Josh. 1.6-7) is echoed here in Haggai's call to this Joshua and all workers, though the Hebrew form in Josh. 1.9 uses a slightly different preposition. The repetition of the imperative 'be strong' called each leader and the community to work harder and not be disappointed with the outcome, for they could not expect their work to compare favourably with the original Temple when they did not have access to the cedar timbers and treasures that were available to Solomon. In fact, it was probably impossible that this collective of workers could even begin to imagine what the old Temple looked like, other than having a general awareness of temple sites, with their altars, courts and sacred spaces. Now, all that lay before them in the rubble were the remnants of stone walls, pillars and an outline of the Temple platform. It looked 'as nothing' to them.

Three times in this verse the concluding formula *'says the Lord'* is added (2.4a, c, d), presumably to emphasize the three imperative forms, 'take courage!' and the call to 'work!' However, there is no sense that the three concluding formulas bring anything to a conclusion following the rhetorical questions in v. 3. (See Appendix A for further discussion of the non-standard use of the messenger formula in Haggai.) Additionally, the final call, 'Work, because I am with you', does not have the same note of generosity about it that the unconditional promise in 1.13 conveyed. Following a command to 'work', the 'promise' takes on a very different tone.

2.5

The promise in 2.4 is seemingly tied to what was seen as the founding event of the nation, that is, God's presence, leading and provisioning, during the Exodus.

The Hebrew text of this verse, however, is problematic. It begins with 'the word' as the direct object of a verb, but the verb is missing. Since the first half of the verse is omitted in the LXX and other ancient versions, there is some level of doubt about the reliability of the verse and the reference to the Exodus. The LXX is at times helpful in settling problems in the Hebrew text, but when a line is missing the challenge to be clear about any intended meaning is great. Additionally, the promise referred to in 2.5a with regard to the people leaving Egypt introduces a new topic that seems to intrude between the promise of divine presence in 2.4 and the parallel promise of the abiding spirit in 2.5b, raising further questions about the text overall. The impression given this reader is that 2.5a is an example of an independent and incomplete statement inexplicably intruding into the text (cf. 1.8), while 2.5b affirms the spirit's presence, in the same way that the 'spirit' in 1.14 was said to accompany the divine presence in 1.13.

If the MT as it currently stands is maintained, then it may be possible to suggest a verb with which the verse may have begun. Unfortunately, commentators' suggestions as to what verb might have been present originally are necessarily subjective and arbitrary, so positing any particular verb to fill the lacuna contributes little to an assured text.

The use in 2.5a of 'the word' (*dābār*, also meaning a matter, or thing), rendered in NRSV and others as 'promise' and linked to leaving Egypt, evokes the narrative of a covenant relationship established between Yahweh and Moses. The allusion to the Exodus narrative is supported by the use of the Hebrew verb *kārat,* 'cut', which is central to the idiom for covenant making; covenants are 'cut', not 'made/entered into'. The idiom reflects the ritual of cutting up a large animal (small animals like birds were not cut up) for sacrifice when sealing a covenant and recalls an early sacrificial model involving Abram (Gen. 15.1-18). These echoes of Yahweh's intimate involvement in the life of the people from its earliest beginnings, stories that were kept alive by being recited at key festival times, meant that the tradition was always very much in the forefront of people's minds. Haggai drew on this to encourage the work to continue.

The second half of the verse, v. 5b, focuses on the work of the 'spirit' again, as in 1.14; 'my spirit' is here parallel to the personal pronoun 'I' and the assurance of the divine presence in 2.4. It was the energizing power that in this case animated or breathed life into the community with a promise that the spirit would remain firm, literally 'standing', within the community. This word was critical to the community re-establishing itself in the land they believed had been promised to them in perpetuity. That confidence had been shattered by the experience of defeat and exile, but with the restoration to the land, Haggai encouraged the people to once again find comfort in the word, the covenant promise of divine presence, by continuing to repair the 'house' in which Yahweh would again dwell.

The final command, 'Fear not', may allude to not being scared, rather than to an act of devotion as is the case in 1.12, for there is evidence in Ezra 4.1-16 that there were adversaries from the Persian province Beyond the River who offered to assist the Temple rebuild, but, when rebuffed, appealed to the new Persian leader, Ahasuerus, for work to be stopped (Ezra 4.24). On the other hand, there is what is arguably another allusion to the cutting of a covenant, as the report of the covenant with Abram in Gen. 15.1 begins with this same comforting word to Abram, 'do not fear'. More generally, throughout the Old Testament and especially typical of Isaiah 40–55, 'do not fear' is a significant introductory form used in reports of encounters with the awesome God.

It is striking to observe that key terms and phrases in 2.4d, 5b, namely 'fear', 'I am with you', and 'spirit' repeat from 1.12d-14. Whether this is by deliberate editorial design or merely a reflection of the editor's personal linguistic range is unclear, but it does add to the sense of the final text attributed to Haggai being brought together as a loose collection of materials rather than as an integrated plot-driven report.

2.6-9

The prophet explains why the people need not be afraid: the Lord of hosts will remain with them and act to provide what is currently lacking, namely treasures that will make this Temple outshine that of Solomon. This promise was grounded in the notion of God as the Lord of hosts, the warrior, with a heavenly army, master of the heavens and ruler of nations and having the power to 'shake' (Hebrew *rʿš*) the cosmos. The use of the title 'Lord of hosts' five times in this section highlights the notion of divine power. Cosmic upheaval, used as a descriptor of power, is a highly coloured motif (see also Joel 3.14-17); the other demonstration of divine power is 'shaking all the nations', though how and what that entails specifically is not spelled out, for the motif or trope is a literary device, a manner of speaking about God and power. All gold and silver are claimed by the Lord, so Israel's God has the right to recover it from the nations for his Temple as the spoils of war.

What are the nations to be shaken? They are the *haggôyîm*, the foreigners—Ammon, Moab, Edom, Aram, Philistia, Tyre, Egypt, even Persia the current dominant empire. Haggai does not explain who they are or what they have done to deserve this shake-up other than their being traditional enemies who have harassed and humiliated Israel and its God in the past. They are not charged here with any explicit evil, but, under the influence of Deuteronomy's xenophobic attitude to the *gôyîm*, Haggai simply stated that they are to be 'shaken' for Judaea's benefit. The view that Yahweh's interaction with the powers of the world is for the particular benefit of his covenant people is the nationalistic perspective that pervades Haggai's outlook.

The promises attributed to Haggai, both here and in 2.21-22, of God 'shaking' the entire created world in order to achieve his purposes derive from Haggai's basic theological platform, his understanding of how God the creator works. Haggai's is an extraordinary vision, expressed in exaggerated language, intended to encourage the people of Jerusalem in their rebuilding work. The shake-up uses the imagery of thunder, lightning, earthquake to initiate a new order. The promise of treasure flowing imminently into Jerusalem exemplifies a prophetic trope that spoke of some undefined divine intervention that should give hope and encouragement to the builders to keep at their task of rebuilding. However, as a trope, the editor simply leaves the promise hanging. There is no answer as to how the promise would actually be realized, only that it would be 'in a little while'.

While one can acknowledge the use of such imagery and inflated language as a literary device, it is possible to wonder what underpinned the notion that the metaphorical 'shaking' might result in the nations (plural—so how many?) being motivated to surrender their treasures, and especially to hand them over to the Judaeans for the Temple decoration. How does shaking and handing over treasures logically connect? The connection would seem to be that the nations would assume (1) that it was Israel's God who caused the shake-up, whatever form it took, and (2) so seek to assuage this foreign God by offering their treasures for his Temple. Such a thought process may well be founded on Haggai's understanding of the Lord of hosts as divine warrior, but a nation will only hand over its treasures as spoil if and when defeated by a more powerful enemy. Here the prophet envisages Judaea's enemies being defeated by Yahweh, the Jewish God, to whom they then willingly offer treasures in acknowledgment of that defeat.

Some commentators refer to the hyperbolic language of 2.6-9, envisioning the nations offering up their treasures to beautify the Temple, as an 'eschatological' promise, meaning that it has to do with 'end times' rather than with any immediate future in 520 BCE. Their suggestion aims to re-interpret the 'treasures' and 'this house' in non-material or figurative terms, and thus seek to sidestep the historic problem of the non-fulfilment of Haggai's expectations. However, the present context and Hebrew syntax make it abundantly clear that the prophet's promise of world-shaking events foresees them as real and as taking place soon, 'in a little while'.

The problem to which this section in particular gives rise is Haggai's focus on the Temple and treasures. What was the purpose of the rebuilding programme? One would be forgiven for thinking that the Temple was a religious centre, the locus of festive worship and daily sacrificial activity, but Haggai does not even express the hope that cultic activity might soon resume. His focus is on treasure, on God acquiring treasures for his glory. He shows no interest in the practicalities and purpose of the rebuilding—no budget plan, no supervisor appointed, no details regarding the Temple as Temple. There is something very odd about the absence of the prophet's interest in cultic matters, one of the more important reasons for having a Temple, even though he is a prophet, not a priest. His major concern was the Temple and its treasures themselves being a means of glorifying God. Haggai obviously did not regard Joshua favourably; he was highly critical of the high priest, whose name now disappears altogether from the document.

The section 2.6-9 offers another example of the non-standard use of the concluding phrase of the messenger form. While there is a beginning phrase, *'Thus says the Lord'* in 2.6, the following verses consist of a series of short claims or promises, each of which ends with the concluding form *'says the Lord'*. Only the final example in 2.9c actually concludes the section. The function of the four concluding forms is presumably to add emphasis to each element of the promise, as is also observable in the second 'shaking' example in 2.21-23, but see Appendix A.

2.6

The opening phrase *'Thus says the Lord of hosts'* is a traditional form that identifies a prophetic message. In this case it is prefaced by a particle (*kî*) that appears to link the following promise with the preceding call, providing the grounds for being fearless. However, it is also possible to read the *kî* particle as 'indeed', an emphatic. The message itself begins with an adverbial phrase in Hebrew that is confusing—both its syntax and possible meanings are widely disputed. However, the general context suggests that it anticipates an imminent event, introducing the theme of a cosmic shake-up, even something currently in progress. The Hebrew root term used (*r'š*) occurs in a number of other contexts, both concrete, as in Amos 1.1 (earthquake), and figuratively as in Isa. 29.6, Jer. 47.3 and Ezek. 38.19.

The LXX omits a translation of the last two Hebrew words, 'the sea and the dry land', so again there is a slight textual issue, though not one of significance for the overall intent of the message. The adverb 'yet' or 'again' can be linked back to the verb 'say', but some link it with the following phrase that is literally 'once a little it is'. It is a long-standing problem textually, and the specific sense is unclear. However, the following statement uses a Hebrew participle that in terms of syntax refers to something happening or about to happen. In other words, the thrust of the wording overall is clearly forward looking, despite there being a minor textual issue.

Haggai's vision that the Lord of hosts is about to 'shake' the entire creation—heavens, earth, sea and land—is another instance of hyperbole, expanding on the highly imaginative language used generally in descriptions of the Day of the Lord and its impact, whether it comes for blessing or judgment, as, for example, in Isa. 13.13 and Joel 1.15. The 'hosts' at Yahweh's command presumably will be the divine agents doing the metaphorical shaking, but what actual form the shake-up is supposed to take is not identified, unless the thought is the same as that in 2.21-22; here it is merely a literary convention, a general way of talking about what Haggai believes will be God's intervention.

Assuming that the reference to the sea (Hebrew *yām*) is textually acceptable, it should be noted that in Canaanite religion Yam was one of the gods, and that perhaps here there is a hint that Yahweh is claiming superiority over local gods of which Yam was one. Israelite religion is often treated as though it were monolithic, but there is enough evidence to demonstrate that popular religion was syncretistic (Josh. 24.14-15) and that 'official' monotheistic religion was often only followed by the religious caste. Yam was known in song (Ps. 29.3-4, 10) and tradition in Israel.

2.7

Enemy nations only give up their treasures to the victor when defeated in battle or in order to buy influence. Surrendering treasure in response to a cosmic shake-up that is attributed to a foreign god, Yahweh, for the glorification of his Temple is hardly to be expected in literal terms. Yet that is what Haggai promised. Haggai presents the treasures as 'coming', without specifying how or when they might come, other than saying that 'I will fill this house', the emphasis being on the divine initiative.

This cosmic upheaval is claimed to impact all the (foreign) nations, meaning all Judah's traditional enemies, the nations that surrounded it, who had recently delivered such defeat to Judah and its God Yahweh. They will be forced now to part with their looted treasures. How that will happen is obviously left unexplained other than it being a divine operation. Ezra 1.6-7 records Cyrus returning the stolen Temple vessels to Sheshbazzar, along with a popular response as people offered other valuables to the returning Jews. This action provided the paradigm for others to make offerings of treasured items. But how would the nations know that any literal shaking (earthquake?) was the work of Israel's God and not their own gods? How would they discern that they should now offer their treasures to Judaea, of all places? Why would they infer that offering their treasured items to Jerusalem will assuage the gods' anger? There is no necessary connection between cosmic shaking and the surrender of treasure to Jerusalem. Haggai's use of this highly metaphoric language, this hyperbole, has no reality behind it, but it conveys to his hearers a message of hope in Yahweh's support, intending to encourage all to keep working and finish the Temple. The exaggerated promise envisions that the 'shaking' will result in much more than just the stolen treasures from Jerusalem being returned (Ezra 1.4); as 2.8 notes, it will be the gold and silver, the precious things, things treasured by Judaea's enemies that Haggai says will be released and brought to Jerusalem. This promised action would demonstrate that Yahweh was honoured by the nations, reversing Israel's and Yahweh's 'defeat' as in the destruction by the enemy of God's 'house' in 587 BCE. According to the prophet, as a result of divine action, God's house will be filled with splendor or glory (Hebrew *kābôd* has a range of values including heaviness, power, honour—e.g. 1 Kgs 8.11), reflecting the power of the Lord of hosts. A gorgeous Temple is for the divine one's enjoyment, as well as exuding a sense of divine power to those who worship at its altar. By means of that gross exaggeration, going far beyond any reality, the prophet attempts to encourage the workers to complete the Temple repair.

Traditionally, the Temple was more than just a worship centre—it also housed the national treasury—see 2 Kgs 12.4, 18. Thus, Haggai's vision was of a restored Temple and treasury, the repository of national wealth rather than a mere worship centre. That was to be its 'glory'.

2.8

Yahweh's claim to ownership of all gold and silver is expressed emphatically: literally, 'to me the silver and to me the gold'. It too is hyperbole. This statement may describe the precious things or 'treasures' in 2.7 that were to be recovered by Yahweh's hosts, claiming them on the basis of an Israelite worldview in which God as creator owns all things. Alternatively, the Hebrew preposition can mean '*for* me the silver and *for* me the gold', in which it speaks more of the silver and gold for making the necessary ritual objects to be used in the Temple rather than being a simple claim for ownership. The language also echoes that of Joel 3.5, which refers to the earlier looting of the Temple's gold, silver and treasures. There are obvious echoes of the Chronicler's description of the 'house of the Lord' in 1 Chronicles 22, with its references to David's hard-won provision of vast amounts of gold and silver, along with other supplies (22.14), his confidence in the divine presence (22.18) and the 'gift' of *shalom*, meaning the absence of conflict. With these and all other necessary items provided in abundance to Solomon, David's call was to 'go and build the sanctuary of the Lord'. For Haggai that model was entirely relevant.

2.9

In contrast to the current ruined state of the Temple (2.3), Haggai envisaged the finished Temple as a marvel—literally 'great will be the glory of this house'. The 'nothing' ruins will become a glorious 'house'. The rather vague expression 'great' can refer to large size, as well as how spectacular or grand it will be. There is also a Jewish suggestion (Rashi) that the promise of greatness was actually fulfilled when this Temple's longevity lasted more years than that of Solomon—from 520 BCE to 70 CE. Haggai's vision was of a Temple of unsurpassed beauty, a place of wonder.

The noun 'glory', a concept related to things that are heavy, weighty, splendid, abundant and dignified, here can be considered to describe both a sense of a powerful divine presence in it, as well as it being magnificently adorned, filled with treasures. Thus, the finished Temple, again using hyperbole, will be greater than the former, that of Solomon. Here the comparison echoes Isa. 41.22 and 42.9 and the language contrasting 'former' and 'latter' situations.

Haggai the divine messenger echoed the scene from 1 Chronicles 22 with a further closing promise: 'And in this place I shall give *shalom*'. This 'place' refers to Jerusalem, city of *shalom*, and in particular to the Temple as the divine dwelling place. The promise is intended to encourage all to continue work on the Temple. In contrast to the current hardships the community faces, God promises 'peace'. It is, of course, a conditional promise dependent on the people taking up and completing the restoration work. Since *shalom* is a very broad concept, embracing people's well-being, harmony, an absence of conflict, it is best understood contextually here as removing the many daily troubles outlined in 1.6-11, that is, leading to a community living in harmony and enjoying bountiful harvests. The NRSV translation of *shalom* as 'prosperity' may be appropriate within the Deuteronomic worldview of material blessings that flow from obedience, the core of its and Haggai's theology. (See 'Theological Ideas' in **Introduction**.) However, it is a concrete example of the translator's conundrum—having to choose one word to render a Hebrew term when that term is multivalent.

The promise is set within the closing formula '*says Yahweh of hosts*', repeated three times to round out the Second Dated Message. On the other uses of the concluding phrase, see Appendix A.

2.10-19 Third Message: December 18, 520 BCE

2.10 On the twenty-fourth day of the ninth month in the second year of Darius the word of the Lord came to Haggai the prophet, saying:

2.11 This is what the Lord of hosts said: 'Ask the priests now [regarding] a torah,

2.12 "If a person carried sanctified meat in his cloak, and the cloak touched some food, the cooked portion, or the wine, or the oil, or anything edible, does it become sanctified?" The priests said, "No!"'

2.13 Then Haggai said: 'If an unclean person touches any of these things, will that make them unclean?'
The priests answered and said: 'he/it is unclean'.

2.14 Haggai then answered: 'This is so with this people, and this is so with this nation before me', says the Lord, 'and thus everything their hands have done and brought there [as an offering] is unclean.'

2.15 'But now ... consider from this day and into the future
Before one stone was placed on another in the Lord's Temple/palace

2.16 [what will be] he came to a heap of twenty and there were ten.
He came to the wine vat to fetch fifty *purah* and there were twenty.

2.17 I struck you and everything you had produced with blight, with mildew and with hail
And/but you were not for me', says the Lord.

100   *Haggai*

2.18 Consider from this day and into the future
      From the twenty-fourth day, from the day in which the Temple of the Lord
      was laid, consider it.
2.19 Is there still the seed in the barn? and yet the vine, the fig tree, the pomegranate, the olive tree bear nothing?
      From this day I will bless you.

There are three separate elements that have been editorially stitched together in this section, the first in 2.10-14 in which Haggai was ordered to ask the priests for clarity on a matter of torah, a question relating to ritual cleanliness. Following the marker 'But now', are the second and third elements, 2.15-17 and 2.18-19, which have a parallel form or construction, and are to be regarded as two separate but superficially conflicting memories of one oral call for people to 'consider' what might be about to happen. They parallel the two 'consider' examples in 1.5-6 and 1.7-9 that look to the present or immediate past.

Two months after the previous message, that is, on December 18, 520 BCE, Haggai is again in receipt of a message, the first of two messages to arrive that day. It required Haggai to ask a series of questions of the priests. The new message, however, differed markedly from that pursued in 2.1-9, having nothing to do directly with the rebuilding work. In 2.10-14 Haggai is moved to ask questions about torah, laws concerning holiness and uncleanness. Priests were responsible for determining whether an object or person was 'clean' or 'unclean', meaning whether people or objects were *ritually* clean and thus could participate in or be used in religious activity or worship. It was not a matter of physical cleanliness or of morality, but rather part of a taboo system that could exclude a person or object, temporarily or permanently, from participation in religious activity. Objects determined to be 'clean' could become contaminated, made unclean, by contact with a dead body or for other reasons (see Lev. 10.10-11; 12.2-5; 13.45-46 etc.). What is peculiar about the divine command given to Haggai is that essentially every member of the community would know the distinction between clean and unclean and how that designation was made. The questioning by Haggai appears then to be an editorial device to introduce a statement about the people and their work as 'unclean'. What is lacking is a connection between the explanation of this particular torah by the priests and the conclusion that Haggai draws from it, with the result that Haggai's analogy in 2.14 simply ends without any meaningful connection to material before or after.

In 2.15-19 the people are challenged again to reflect seriously on their situation. Three times they are challenged to 'consider' (2.15, 18a, 18d), and to do so with regard to the impending future, 'from this day forward'

(2.15b, 18a, 19c). The focus here is again on the hardship and food shortages that continued to be a feature of their lives, and on the people's alleged failure to respond to Yahweh (2.17). The concluding promise is that Yahweh will bless the people and the harvest failure will be turned around, echoing language similar to that used by Joel (Joel 2.18-19). God is said to promise a blessing, but there is no accompanying requirement for a change in the people's attitude. The promise itself seems almost an afterthought.

There are also questions in the section 2.10-19 having to do with its unity: (1) is the abrupt ending at 2.14 that fails to explain or clarify how Haggai drew such a conclusion from the priests' response to his questions; (2) the discourse marker 'but now' at 2.15 and the imperative call to 'consider' the future that suddenly takes the editorial report into a new direction altogether.

2.10-14 A Priestly Ruling on Holiness and Haggai's Application

Once again the divine word is said to have come to Haggai. This was the first of two messages on that day, December 18, 520 BCE. The first came with an order for the prophet to ply the priests with several questions and have them make a ruling. The text again makes clear that it is God who prompted Haggai to ask these questions, but the purpose for asking seems opaque, to say the least.

The issue of concern that apparently requires Haggai to ask the question is a curious one in the sense that it was normally common knowledge in the community as to what constituted 'cleanliness'. This was especially so with regard to anything or anyone touching a dead body. Does it imply that the community had forgotten the relevant rules given that offering sacrifices at the Temple had been in abeyance for seventy and more years? Did they need reminding of the principles surrounding acceptable worship? What purpose was served by having Haggai seek clarification of the issue? It was not for his benefit or enlightenment, surely!

The priests who were asked to clarify the matter for Haggai are not identified, but Ezra 3.36-38 states that over three thousand of them returned to Jerusalem in 538 BCE. Although the number sounds excessive, and the responsibility of a community supporting that number of priests, if accurate, would have been a huge burden, the primary task of the priest was in instructing the people in torah, the applied regulations, as well as ensuring that all knew well the national story. Why Haggai did not enquire of Joshua as high priest for a simple ruling is unknown, though it is clear that Joshua, who was criticized by Haggai for failing to advance the rebuilding, disappears altogether from the editor's report after 2.4! Had he died? Or was he ignored for other reasons?

The questions asked of the priests relate to a 'clean' object, one that had been examined and agreed by the priests to have been unblemished and thus acceptable for offering; could such an object be rendered 'unclean'? Could contact with something 'clean' make the 'unclean' clean? It was a very basic question to which all should have known the answer. The priests gave their unequivocal response, as expected: unclean things can make clean things unfit for cultic use. Haggai takes that unsurprising response and applies it by way of analogy to the people and their work: they and all their work are 'unclean'. The ramifications of this conclusion are unexplained, and the editor drops the subject and switches to a completely new topic in v. 15.

2.10-11

Here a third date in Darius's second year is given—ninth month, twenty-fourth day, or December 18, 520 BCE. The editor records it as the moment Haggai received the first of two messages that day from the Lord of hosts. The text states that the word came to Haggai 'saying: *Thus says the Lord of hosts*: "Ask the priests . . ."' This is an awkward construction in which the introductory element in the messenger form is redundant (also the closing element '*says the lord*' is misplaced!), such that it can be read as a message for the prophet to require others to ask questions of the priests. The issue is whether 'Ask the priests' is the content of the message to Haggai as messenger, or the content of what he is to pass on to an audience to have them ask the questions. Despite this issue, the rest of the interaction makes clear that it was Haggai himself who was to ask the priests for clarification of the torah regarding the transmission of uncleanness, that is, food taboos. The topic is unrelatable to any other matter said to have concerned Haggai at the time. So, both the syntax and the topic leave the reader wondering what was the point being made, unless one accepts that the editor has simply used the question and answer as a way to introduce Haggai's apparent conclusion that the people and their achievements are somehow 'unclean' (2.14).

The prophet did not need to seek a priest's authoritative answer to these basic questions, for the taboo around objects and persons and clean/unclean matters was integral to community religious life. The taboo was understood by most, if not all. Furthermore, the issue had no connection to the Temple repair problem, and Haggai's application by analogy in v. 14 is far from informative. So, both the questions and the response are independent of the earlier context, suggesting that the issue may well represent a random memory of a separate oral tradition associated with Haggai. There is no obvious answer to the question of the significance of the encounter with the priests.

Questions were the specific literary form that the editor has imposed on each of the dated communications in 1.4, 2.3, and now here in 2.11-13, and later in 2.19. Observing this editorial pattern helps explain the editor's means of presenting the prophet's message overall but does not explain the subject of clean/unclean objects itself or its implications. It is a genuine conundrum.

2.12

The matter of clean and unclean items, or food taboos, is the focus. A sanctified piece of meat carried in one's pocket (literally, the fold of one's garment) may brush against some other food item whether in the Temple or at one's home. Can the sanctified meat sanctify by touch that other item, that is, make it something now acceptable for sacrifice? According to priestly tradition, torah, the answer is: No, it cannot make it 'clean'. No matter the type of food, be it bread, cooked meat, wine, or oil, none can be made ritually clean by coming into contact with the sanctified meat. Leviticus 7.14-19 makes clear that sanctified food of a special well-being offering of unleavened cakes, unlike certain other offerings, can be reserved and eaten the day following the sacrificial rite if not all of it was consumed on the occasion of its offering. This would mean that the food could be taken home in the fold or pocket of whatever garment one was wearing. It was required to be kept free of contact with anything considered unclean in order to retain its sanctified or holy state. The Hebrew concept of holiness was not a matter of morality; that which was 'holy' was something or someone set apart for some special purpose, dedicated to God. In this particular context, an animal that was unblemished and had been dedicated to God, set apart for that specific use and no other, was holy in whole and in part, but it could not make another item holy or clean. Ritual holiness was not transferable, and every offering required priestly certification. On the other hand, ritual uncleanness *was* transferable, as the answer to the second question made plain. Touching a dead body automatically renders that object or person defiled. These were two of the most basic torah statements in Israel's religious world.

2.13

Haggai's second question, a correlate of 2.12, asks about a possible case in which an individual made contact, for whatever reason, with a dead body, an 'unclean *nepeš*'. The Hebrew noun *nepeš* normally refers to something living, as in Gen. 2.7, but here appears to refer to a corpse, as in Num. 5.2;

9.6-7. Thus the person who was temporarily ritually defiled and who then touched food rendered that food unclean (see Lev. 21.11; 22.4); it could not be offered to God. Uncleanness or contamination is transferable; holiness or cleanness, not so. Again, it is a matter of which most people of the time would be aware. These were not questions Haggai needed to ask to obtain information of which he was ignorant, so what was the purpose in asking? It is possible to think of the questions serving as an editorial device to report Haggai's alleged negative attitude toward the entire community, what he considered its loss of ritual fitness.

2.14

Under the guise of receiving an answer to his questions, Haggai applied the priest-defined principles with regard to uncleanness, announcing that the people and their work and whatever they offered have become 'unclean'. What is lacking is any explanation of how the torah of food becoming unclean was applied to the people, their work, and what they brought as an offering. The verb phrase 'what they bring near', an idiomatic use of the verb 'come near', referring to the offering of sacrifices, is in the form that indicates frequent or regular activity.

As the text stands, it was Haggai who declared that all was 'unclean'. Since clean/unclean decisions rested with the priests and not with prophets, Haggai was not qualified to determine anything to be clean or unclean. It is obvious therefore that Haggai is using the 'unclean' designation metaphorically rather than literally. At a rhetorical level, three components considered unclean are individually identified: literally, '*thus* this people, and *thus* this nation, . . . and *thus* all the work of their hands', along with their sacrifices. The uncleanness analogy was applied to 'every work of their hands', a phrase that is so broad as to include all work, no matter what trade, business, or agricultural work the community undertook. It was also a very Deuteronomic phrase (Deut. 2.7; 31.29; 33.11). The food analogy itself was irrelevant to the basic matter of Temple repair, and Haggai's metaphorical application to a vague 'everything' is never defined more closely, and certainly never resolved.

If Haggai's analogy referred to actual ritual uncleanness rather than a metaphorical one, it would have been possible, theoretically, for the priests to declare a way of restoring ritual cleanliness. Ensuring cleanliness within the community was an important priestly responsibility. If the uncleanness was temporary, lasting until the evening, it could have been resolved by ritual washing or shaving (Lev. 14.7-8). If it was an enduring uncleanness, as seems implied in this case, then other steps could have been taken to resolve the problem. The priests who were present could have offered

Haggai a solution to ensure that ritual cleanliness was re-established in the community, and that they, their work and offerings that had become contaminated, could be sanctified. However, nothing was done to rectify whatever problem Haggai had in mind.

For some commentators, the 'unclean' element refers to the Samaritans who offered to participate in the reconstruction of the Temple. Their participation could have meant that the Judaeans and the entire project had become contaminated. Haggai's lack of explanation for his analogy has led some to assume, contrary to the metaphor, that it is the unrestored Temple itself that was regarded as unclean, having been defiled by invading foreigners. If it was unclean, Haggai's response raises an awkward question: If the Temple was contaminated, and now also the people and their work and offerings, how could it be remedied such that the restoration work might be carried out? Is it a case of an unclean Temple making the people unclean, or unclean people making the Temple unclean? There is no resolution in this approach.

Other attempts to make sense of the 'uncleanness' charge are equally unhelpful. For example, one suggestion is that the people did not honour God, or that God was upset at seeing the destruction of the Temple and the desecration of its altar, so things offered there were not acceptable to God. This attempt at an explanation presents a serious problem, since it was Yahweh who brought in the Babylonians to destroy the Temple in the first place. Or was it that syncretistic worship by some involved in the work defiled all that was done there. Attempts at explanation are not based in evidence, and so are unconvincing. Some have argued for a contrast between 'this people' (Hebrew *hā'ām-hazzeh*) and 'this nation' (Hebrew *haggôy hazzeh*) as referring to two distinct groups, the former referring to 'clean' Judaeans and the latter referring to 'unclean' foreign or Samaritan offers of involvement in the restoration work. Although *gôy* normally means a foreign person, the more likely explanation of the two phrases is that they are a hendiadys; no ethnic or tribal distinction is intended, both referring to the community of residents in and around Jerusalem.

What one has to consider is the possibility that the editor has omitted material that would clarify the report or has worked with an oral version that was itself incomplete. Another possibility is that during the transmission process, the ending of the report was lost. Whatever the solution, 2.10-14 is an incomplete or truncated report that leaves Haggai's analogy without explanation and, more importantly, without resolution. It is a case of never knowing what was intended by this questioning and the prophet's application, and a warning to commentators not to make too much of an incomplete text.

The text of 2.10-14 is further evidence that this third-person report contains incomplete and disconnected inserts (see also 1.8; 2.5cd; 2.19d). Haggai's editor was at some distance removed from the prophet himself, and what he reported was based on disparate and incomplete oral material available to him at the time.

The report then moves via a significant transitional marker, 'but now', to another matter altogether, to a call to reflect on or 'consider' the future (2.15-17, 18-19).

2.15-19 Two Calls to Reflect on the Future

A new subsection begins without the traditional messenger form, but with the introductory, 'And now . . . from this day on'. It marks an abrupt transition to a situation altogether unrelated to the clean and unclean question in 2.10-14; it has absolutely no connection or relevance to any priestly concerns. The priests are no longer dialogue partners, and the focus shifts back to the community and its future. Three times in the following verses, 2.15-19, there is a call for the people to 'consider' their present experience. These are combined with the phrase 'from this day on' that forms an inclusion for the subsection, ending with a simple promise of blessing. Haggai is presented as speaking for Yahweh with first-person address; however traditional speech formulas that note that the prophet was speaking on God's behalf do not open and close this section.

This section constitutes the most problematic one for the interpreter due to (1) issues in the Hebrew text; (2) two separate calls to 'consider', with no specific demand for people to change priorities and work to restore the Temple; (3) two references to Temple building or repair, and (4) a call to 'return' that is of dubious provenance. Despite these challenges, which will be dealt with individually below, there is an overall sense that Haggai was calling the people to reflect on the past harvest shortfalls that God had imposed, with the intention, according to the editor, of spurring the people to change their priorities.

While most commentators regard the relationship between 2.15-17 and 2.18-19 to be sequential, the view being advocated here is that they are actually two variant versions of one and the same prophetic comment. From the point of view of structure: (1) both begin with the formal call to 'consider . . . from this day on' (2.15a, 18a); (2) both then describe the agricultural devastation brought on by God (2.16-17, 19a). The first call notes God's intention in calling the drought, a plan that appears to have failed to result in people 'returning' to God, and the second, using rhetorical questions (as in 1.4; 2.3, 12-13), pointing out that there is currently no grain or fruit remaining (2.19ab). The editor then adds a conclusion (3), an independent promise of blessing (2.19c). That promise does not outline any basis or conditions for such blessing. Both versions of the prophet's comment independently recall a connection to the Temple building or to its foundation. The suggestion that these are two variant versions of a single comment by Haggai resolves the problem of a supposed sequential relationship between 2.15-17 and 2.18-19 by recognizing that the editor has included differing versions or memories of a call by Haggai to think of the future. While Haggai most probably spoke numerous times in the same vein, the editor has made no attempt to solve the apparent conflict in the references to Temple building (2.15) or foundation laying (2.18); he simply included both.

The blessing promised in 2.19c is a fully independent and unrelated statement that is appended to the section by means of the inclusion phrase 'from this day on' to conclude the third dated report. It is, however, closely related to the Deuteronomic perspective of material 'blessing', which in this context had to mean that all that was lacking will be restored.

The lack of clarity within the text of 2.15-19 signals something of the difficulty faced by an editor when confronted with multiple oral versions circulating within the community. The gap between the assumed original presentation(s) by the prophet and the oral report(s) of his message that followed that occasion, and any repeated calls he made, were eventually collected by a literate editor for memorializing. It was inevitable that variations defying easy reconciliation circulated orally for lengthy periods among a prophet's supporters, and there is no way to tell how long the material circulated before being set in writing (see 'Dating Haggai' in the **Introduction**). These facts typify the oral environment in which this and most other prophetic material evolved.

Here in 2.15-19 we have one such example: two versions of a single message, whether varied by the prophet in his own representations on different occasions or varied in the sharing within the community. The result is that slightly differing references to Temple-building activity have been set alongside each other without reconciling them. Further complication is evident in the appended reference to the objective of the God-induced crisis, namely, that the people 'return' to God, based on an enigmatic text of an idea arguably attributable to Zechariah, not to Haggai (see below).

2.15-17 'Consider . . .' III

The introductory 'But now' marks a transition in the presentation, as it did in 1.5 and 2.4, to an imperative, another call to 'consider' a present circumstance, but here with a view to some future event or situation. This call is clearly a significant element in what the editor sees as Haggai's challenge to the people, a way of drawing their attention to a situation from which lessons are to be learned. The form used in this verse is identical to that found in 2.18, suggesting that it is a fixed form at least for the editor, especially as both examples end with the same Hebrew phrase *mā'lâ*, the meaning of which is unfortunately unclear. That final phrase, rendered as 'what will come to pass' (NRSV), appears to derive from a root word *'lh*, which regularly conveys an upward movement but in a temporal reference may point to the future (see 1 Sam. 30.25), though some have seen it as looking backward. One point that can be appreciated is the wordplay using the verb *śym*, 'put, place': the people are called to 'put their hearts' or 'consider' matters, as the stones are 'put' one on top of the other. It is probably a clever literary feature rather than having some deeper significance, but one can never be sure.

Questions surrounding the correct Hebrew text of this verse continue as the time phrase rendered as 'before' (*mitterem*, literally, 'from beginning') occurs nowhere else, leaving readers without examples with which to compare and clarify it. The phrase would appear to refer to an early or initial time when there was an attempt to 'put one stone on another' in the Temple, but it is such a vague descriptor that it could apply to an original building work or to subsequent repair work that was current. The use of the timeless infinitive of the verb 'put' refers back to an earlier action, supposedly the period before the repair work had begun. While the lack of food supply before they began repairing the Temple remained unchanged, from this moment on, Haggai says they can expect better things. Haggai's statement serves as encouragement to keep the repair work going.

Perhaps surprisingly, Haggai refers to the ruined building as a 'Temple' (Hebrew *hēykāl*) rather than a 'house'. If he is pointing back to the building that was there originally, then this may be appropriate.

The Hebrew text proceeds with a phrase *mihyôtām*, marked by the Masoretes as belonging to the following 2.16. It is, however, a problematic phrase, with a possible meaning 'from their being', or 'before their being', reading the initial *mem* as the preposition 'from' attached to the participle of the verb 'be' that carries a third-person suffix. The phrase seems to have little meaning of itself unless seen as beginning 2.16 and relating to the way matters stood before the repair work began. Some have suggested emending the text following the LXX and giving a possible meaning such as 'what were you?' or 'who were you?'

2.16

There is a general consensus that the problem phrase 'from/before their being', which the text associates with 2.15, is actually something like the

Haggai 2   109

question 'how did you fare?', as in 1.5, 7 and associated with the call to reflect on the past. Despite the fact that the Hebrew in 1.5 and here in 2.15-16 is so different—'put your heart/thought' as against 'from their being'—many translations deem it to mean 'what was the situation?' or similar.

This is a good place to consider that one of the realities of dealing with an ancient language and its record is that on many occasions we modern readers have no idea what a text might mean, either because our understanding of the language and idiom is limited, even with context, or because the record itself is garbled, with mistakes made due to copyists' inattention, or indistinct lettering resulting from centuries of hand copying in older and worn manuscripts. (The following verse will also raise a similar issue with regard to 'return to me'.)

Haggai 2.16 then continues with the two examples of grain and wine shortfalls: the focus is on the quantity of food and drink available, on the gap between what was expected and what little was actually found to be in store. It clearly relates to the 'much–little' theme, as in 1.6, 9.

A 'heap of twenty measures' does not identify the item nor the specific measure involved. 'Heap' as a classifier is hardly an accurate descriptor of an amount, so neither the particularity of the crop nor the specific amount is the primary focus. One can assume it was a grain crop of some kind, perhaps corn or barley being the more common. Expecting that there were twenty measures, people discovered that there were only ten; the yield from the crop was only half what was expected; it is this relative amount that is the point being made. In the case of the wine, the wine that was in storage was short—no longer 50 (measures) available, only a mere 20. The specific liquid measure is not indicated in the text. The impact of the God-ordered drought on the basic food needs of the community, a divine 'strike' according to the prophet, was severe.

2.17

The cause of the shortfall in stored supplies was divine action against the people and their crops. The verb 'struck' speaks of a deliberate act to undermine the community's food production by means of blight, mildew and hail. Drought conditions causing blight and, at other times, too much moisture generating mould, along with occasional hailstorms, were each examples of changing and adverse weather conditions similar to those noted in 1.10-11. While these and similar challenges face all farmers everywhere, agriculture of all types being so weather dependent, Haggai insists that on this occasion the crisis was driven by hostile divine intervention. This was the prophet's interpretation or explanation for a series of complex weather events that were and would always be a feature of life in Judaea, making for an unpredictable harvest year after year. Attributing these, and similar events, to Yahweh's deliberate action is the significant element that lay at the core of Haggai's ideology, though here he makes no attempt to justify God's launch of such an attack. The language used in this reference echoes the words of Solomon's prayer at the dedication of the Temple in 1 Kgs 8.22-53. (See 'Theological Ideas' in the **Introduction**.)

The brief Hebrew phrase *'eyn 'etkem 'ēlî*, literally, 'there is not (with) you to me', if textually correct, has been understood to call for a 'return'. While this is an enigmatic and awkward expression and thus of questionable meaning, it has been taken to imply that the people had failed to respond appropriately to something adverse that God had brought upon them. They allegedly failed to respond appropriately despite there being what Haggai implies was a discernable divine purpose evident in the shortfall. However, there is nothing in the report by the editor that can be considered the prophet's warning to the people that this had been the divine plan prompting the strike; Haggai has not identified specific sins that require them to 'turn back' in the sense of repenting of a sin. To presume that Haggai previously had said more about a divine purpose than is here reported by the editor is baseless. Furthermore, prophetic calls to 'turn back' or 'return' to God traditionally use the Hebrew verb *šûb* (see Hos. 12.6; 14.1; Joel 2.12-13; Amos 4.6, 8, 9, 10, 11). The absence of this key marker verb and the lack of clarity in the enigmatic Hebrew phrase 'not you to me' means that to assume a reference to 'turning' of any kind, and especially as repentance, is completely unwarranted. What is additionally important to note here is that Zechariah, supposedly just one month earlier than Haggai's call (Zech. 1.1-6), challenged the current generation in Jerusalem not to follow what he described as the ancestors' evil ways but to 'turn around' or 'return' to obedience. In this call, Zechariah used the key verb *šûb*, 'turn back', a clear reference to repentance. Concern for repentance and a turnaround were essential parts of Zechariah's demands; Haggai did not make any such call at any point, it appears. Suggesting that the enigmatic phrase in 2.17 is a call by Haggai for all to 'return' or repent, is unsupportable, lacking all evidence. If there was any challenge in December 520 BCE for Judaeans to 'return', it was the message of Haggai's contemporary Zechariah (Zech. 1.1-6) and certainly not of Haggai!

If—and it's a big 'if'—the enigmatic Hebrew in 2.17 can be demonstrated to infer a 'return', a repentance the people failed to achieve, it stemmed from the editor being confused about elements in the advice unique to each of the two prophets. Haggai and Zechariah were simultaneously active in Jerusalem; both were addressing the same cohort living in the same stressful circumstances, but each had their individual concerns, ideology and relevant messages. It is not at all surprising that their oral messages could and would at times become entangled in people's minds, with the special concerns of one attributed to the other as the oral messages circulated throughout the community. A more reasonable explanation for the unusual and opaque syntax of the Haggai text is that an editorial or copyist error has intruded at some point along the transmission line resulting in Zechariah's message being wrongly associated with Haggai. A translation of Hag. 2.17b would be best advised to retain a literal rendering of the problematic Hebrew, place it within brackets and add a footnote explaining the problem with its possible solution.

2.18-19 'Consider . . .' IV

The section opens with a repetition of the call to 'consider' and offers a second version of the prophet's challenge in 2.15-17. The call is dated, as was the introduction to this third communication report, namely, ninth month, twenty-fourth day. There follows the statement that it was from 'the day that the foundation of the Temple of Yahweh was laid'. Commentators have noted an apparent sequencing conflict with the wording of 2.15b in which 'laying one stone on another' appears to refer to building activity that would have taken place *after* the foundation laying, the focus noted in 2.18. There is also some apparent conflict with Ezra 3 and its reference to laying the foundation stone, perhaps in 537 BCE shortly after the return from Babylon. Many attempts have been made to resolve the alleged sequence 'problem', discussing how many foundation stones there might have been in addition to the one original foundation stone, but there is no consensus. Treating the two 'consider' challenges as independent and variant versions of the one call placed alongside each other offers a way to approach the issue, if not resolve it.

2.19

The basic challenge in this verse is how to read what begins with the interrogative particle, the question marker: does the marker serve the entire clause 2.19ab, or is 2.19b a statement following an initial question in 2.19a? The syntax is ambiguous, and commentators and translations adopt a variety of possible solutions to the cryptic Hebrew, 'Still/yet seed in the granary?'

There is no doubting that the verse opens with a question, the literary form chosen by the editor as the medium for presenting Haggai's message throughout. If it asks rhetorically and a negative answer is expected, then it makes the point that there is no seed remaining in the barn, but why that should be the case is not explained; there is no suggestion here that God has caused the loss, if that is what it is. It just might be that, due to a shortfall, there is now nothing remaining in the barn as it was all consumed, or that so much of the small harvest was consumed that there is little left. If it is not a rhetorical question, then both 'yes' and 'no' answers are possible. Similarly, the second part of the verse, if not a second question, is a simple statement that there is no fruit left on the fruit trees. Two scenarios can be imagined: the trees failed to bear any fruit for reasons not indicated—frost destroyed the early buds?; alternatively, what little fruit there was had all been harvested and eaten. On the other hand, if 2.19b continues the opening question form, 'yes' or 'no' is a possible response. The ambiguity has to be settled on grounds other than grammar and syntax, but there is no certainty, only possibilities: (1) both questions are rhetorical; (2) the first is a rhetorical question and the second a statement; (3) both parts are statements. A survey of Bible translations will show that all possibilities are represented.

The position adopted in this commentary is that both v. 19a and v. 19b are parallel as rhetorical questions. This means that (1) the initial question marker serves both parts of the verse, that (2) the opening Hebrew adverb *'ôd* should be read in place of the second question's *'ad,* that is, both ask whether there is 'still' any grain or fruit remaining, and (3) that in the context of the divine 'strike' against the community, the response to the questions is negative. The note at the close of the question form— Hebrew *lo' nāśā',* 'has not borne', (NRSV 'yield nothing')—is much clearer as a negative, though that is almost certainly hyperbole, better understood as meaning there was essentially nothing, or very little food, wine or oil left. In other words, both v. 19a and v. 19b make the point that the barns are virtually empty and the fruit trees have produced little such that currently the community's food needs are in crisis mode. The orientation of the section as a whole, however, anticipates a better future.

The final clause in 2.19c, 'from this day I will bless (you)', is clearly an independent statement, a view supported by the Hebrew mid-sentence marker (*athnaq*) that precedes it; it has no direct connection with the questions that dominate 2.19ab and is not dependent on the preceding or following material, nor is there an explanation for the sudden change in the divine attitude from striking to blessing. Concluding that the people repented of some sin and are now to be blessed, as some have done, is unjustifiable when there is no supporting evidence in this document to indicate that the people and their leaders require repentance. How, then, might one regard the 'promise'? If one assumes that the community has begun to make repairs to the Temple (1.14), responding to Haggai's challenge, then that in itself became the grounds for a promise of blessing. Haggai initially interpreted the poor harvest and food shortages as evidence of divine displeasure with the community's priorities; now, the beginning of repair work had become the basis for the promise of better times—a positive response to the call for Temple repair, that is, real action, would lead to blessings in line with the promises of Deut. 7.12-13, notably a good harvest.

2.20-23 Fourth Message: December 18, 520 BCE

A Future for Judaea under Zerubbabel

2.20   The word of the Lord (came) a second time to Haggai on the twenty-fourth day of the month.
2.21   'Say to Zerubbabel the governor: "I am about to shake the heavens and the earth.
2.22   And I will overturn the thrones of the kingdoms and destroy the strength of those kingdoms,
And overturn the chariot with its driver, and the horses with their riders will fall, each by the sword of his brother."'
2.23   'In that day', *says the Lord of hosts*,
'I will take you Zerubbabel son of Shealtiel, my servant', *says the Lord*,
'and I will appoint you to be like a signet, for you I have chosen', *says the Lord of hosts*.

A second word to Haggai from God is dated December 18, 520 BCE. The message moves away completely from the harvest shortfall and other themes such as the Temple restoration in order to focus on Zerubbabel himself and a future role. It is framed by traditional editorial phrases—'the word of the Lord came . . . to Haggai', closing with three applications of the concluding element of the messenger form '*says the Lord of hosts*' in 2.23, presumably for emphasis—to mark it off as a discrete unit without any context other than a date. It re-uses the 'shaking' theme of 2.6-7. This was a word for Zerubbabel alone; Joshua is no longer Haggai's concern. Whether Joshua was still alive, or had died, is unknown, but it is clear that Haggai had little regard at any point for the high priest and saw no future for him.

The editor reports on this encounter in terms of God commanding Haggai to speak privately to Zerubbabel, here honoured with the title 'my servant', with a promise that God was about to 'shake the heavens and earth'. The shaking imagery used in Haggai has become a trope in the editorial reporting that marks divine action against the nations and their armies on Judaea's behalf. In 2.6-7 the shaking is said to result in treasures flowing into Jerusalem for the Temple project, but here it anticipates the overthrow of nations and their armies. It then combines with a 'day [of the Lord]'

114   *Haggai*

promise to Zerubbabel that he will be made 'like a signet', because God has 'chosen' him. The theme of the unit is such that the previous critical attitude of Haggai toward Zerubbabel is no longer evident. So, what did Zerubbabel make of this new encounter? It certainly seems surprising in view of Haggai's now very positive attitude to the governor. What might have accounted for this sudden and major change of heart?

Recognizing this brief section as using hyperbole is not problematic; readers can identify the device readily. The real issue comes when interpreting the promise in 2.23; is it to be understood literally as many do, and see Zerubbabel as actually becoming the dominant regional ruler, even a messianic figure? Had he done so, there would have surely been more to report. Whatever the promise offered, whether literal or figurative, it would not happen until 'that day', pushing any potential fulfilment into the distant future. The intention or vision behind Haggai's promise is never clarified, however, because the editor falls silent once having reported what Haggai said.

2.20

The word of the Lord awakens Haggai a second time on December 18, 520 BCE. What significance a second interruption held is unclear. The editor has reported this totally unexpected message from Haggai, a message so different from all other material in the report, lacking all connection with Temple rebuilding, priestly concerns, and weaponized Nature leading to the ongoing crisis. It stands as a separate report, presumably based on one of Haggai's messages of which the editor was aware, one that exceeded in significance his other messages, given its implications.

2.21-22

The word from the Lord directed a very personal message to Zerubbabel, the governor. It clearly was not directed at the community, but the editor shared news of the encounter between Haggai and Zerubbabel, raising implications for them as a community if Zerubbabel was ever to embody the promise of regional power that Haggai conveyed.

The message adopted the same hyperbolic imagery of 'shaking' the nations noted in 2.6-7, though in a slightly more brief form. Previously, shaking up the heavens and nations was to humiliate the nations with such obvious demonstrations of divine power that they offered their treasures for Judaea to use in its Temple furnishings (2.7); this time the shake-up goes much further—it will not just shake loose the gold and silver of national treasuries but strip away those nations' power, their royal leadership and military assets.

Haggai 2

The goal of this shaking of the heavens and earth is said to be the destruction of those who rule the nations opposed to God and his people, implying, among other things, that Persian rule would come to an end and Judaea rise to take its place. The imagery conveys a sense of overwhelming divine power rather than offering a literal description of a massive cosmic storm or an earthquake. It employs 'Day of the Lord' imagery, assuring Zerubbabel that God will dethrone kings and destroy the power of empires and their armies. By specifying the 'shaking' imagery in terms of destroying nations and their armies, their chariots and horses, the language mimics that of the defeat of the Egyptian chariots, overthrowing horses and their riders at the Reed Sea (Exod. 14.26-31; 15.1, 21), appropriate imagery when Egypt was the neighbour on the southern flank. The notion that Israel's enemies will turn on each other and self-destruct is another familiar theme of God-inspired victory (Judg. 7.22; Ezek. 38.21). Twice here the editor used the verb 'overthrow' or 'overturn' to express divine power over Judaea's enemies. The language of promise continues to feature hyperbole and should be understood for what it is, traditional rhetoric about divine power and action.

Zerubbabel, unlike Haggai, was not just sympathetic with Persian policy and administration of the province; he was the one implementing those policies. (See 'On Haggai, Zerubbabel and Joshua' in the **Introduction**.) If, as seems clear, Persian dominance coming to an end was implied in Haggai's words, Zerubbabel may have been deeply troubled, or at least taken aback, by this new message from Haggai. It is presented by the editor as coming without warning and without context, making a reasonable interpretation of its meaning more difficult. However, it is the climactic words of the final verse—'*you* I have chosen'—that brings the most serious challenge for the governor. If realized, Haggai's promise would certainly spell the end of his role as Persia's representative.

The promise in 2.21-22 speaks of the destruction of kingdoms and their armies that must imply the end of Persia as well as other nations, and thus of Zerubbabel's Persia-derived authority. It then offered Zerubbabel a very different kind of authority to the one he currently held, that of being 'like a signet' (2.23).

2.23

A phrase found throughout the prophetic material more broadly is 'on that day' (Hos. 2.16; Joel 3.1, 18; Amos 8.9). Here that phrase is inserted and employed similarly, meaning, a divine intervention at some unspecified but imagined point in the future. It signals divine rescue/salvation, or alternatively, punishment, depending on the context. In cases of prophetic warnings and calls for repentance, the 'day' threatens judgment and punishment; but if the warnings were heeded, then that 'day' became a time of rescue from some crisis. Elsewhere 'that day' was known also as 'the Day of the Lord' and commonly associated with prophetic oracles warning of punishment for the sinful and/or salvation for those who repented. When used in the international context, the 'day' was potentially one of rescue for Israel while effecting judgment or punishment on its enemies. The language surrounding the 'day' draws on a wide variety of imagery such as natural calamities (e.g. Joel 1.15-18; 2.10-11, 30), military defeat (Joel 2.10-11), personal danger (Amos 5.18-20) and warfare (Mic. 5.10-15) to portray the overwhelming power of God effecting his will and purpose on both Israel and the nations. In using this phrase, Haggai recalled that broad prophetic vision of a brighter future for his people under God. Zerubbabel would be appointed to a new role.

Generally speaking, 'on that day' refers to an unspecified time in the future; it could be relatively soon, but more commonly it referred to a possibility many, many years into the future, and to that extent, constituted a very vague promise, leaving much room for speculation. The phrase immediately raises a question about the nature of the promise and how it was viewed by both Haggai and Zerubbabel. While it expressed Haggai's hope for some new kind of authoritative leadership from the governor, the report offered no further clarification, and the document simply ends.

Zerubbabel is no longer attached to his title 'governor' here; he is now God's 'servant'. This term 'servant' is one redolent with meaning. From Abraham (Gen. 26.24) to Moses (Deut. 34.5) to Joshua (Judg. 2.8) to David (2 Sam. 3.18; 1 Kgs 11.34) to prophets in general (2 Kgs 17.13), the term carried special significance as identifying those who served their God. In the centrepiece of the Isaianic material, Isaiah 40–55, lies the mission of the Servant of the Lord, God's chosen one. Whether the Servant there was an individual or the collective Israel, it was the Servant who was chosen as God's agent. Zechariah, Haggai's contemporary in Jerusalem, uses the term to refer to one called the 'Branch', possibly an allusion to a potential Davidic role for Zerubbabel (Zech. 3.8). Complicating the issue here is that Jer. 27.6 uses the same term 'servant', applying it to Nebuchadnezzar, so it was a term that could be applied to any who served God's purposes whether Jew or foreigner. It is this basic principle of servanthood, of service, that was evoked in this call to Zerubbabel. For the governor, that service was then defined: he was to become 'like a signet'. The general promise of Zerubbabel's some-day elevation, being 'taken' and 'put in place' like a signet, was based on the prophet's belief that God had 'chosen' him. The combination of these three verbs in this verse makes for a dramatic scenario.

Despite the fact that Haggai at no point refers to Zerubbabel's possible Davidic ancestry, many have read this note to indicate some kind of messianic implications being attached to the governor. Three times in the verse the formal phrase *'says Yahweh of hosts'* is added to underscore the importance of each component of the promise (see Appendix A). The prophet claims that Zerubbabel is to be made *'like* a signet (ring)', a simile, that he would be like one holding a position of authority (see Jer. 22.24, where the signet or authority is stripped from Jehoiachin, Zerubbabel's grandfather). Note that Zerubbabel is *not* the signet but only likened to one. The significance of that simile should not be over-interpreted, or, dare it be said, not under-interpreted. A signet was a token of royal or official dignity and authority, but the metaphor was also used in love poems (see Song 8.6) to speak of commitment and belonging. Jehoiachin, Judah's last king, was described in Jer. 22.24 as the signet (ring) on Yahweh's right hand. There is no necessary royal or Davidic association implicit in being a seal or signet; what it speaks of is 'belonging'. So, what did Haggai actually mean when speaking of the governor being like a signet? What can be said about this promise is that Haggai was full of hope that Zerubbabel would fill a significant role because he believed him to be 'chosen'.

What might Zerubbabel's response or reaction have been to the promise that he was chosen to become such a regional power? The Hebrew syntax puts special emphasis on the personal—*you* I have chosen! Haggai's deliberate use of the notion of Zerubbabel being someone 'chosen' (see Deut. 4.37-40; 7.6; 10.15) reflects his theological background. However, there is much to suggest that Zerubbabel, if he accepted the notion at all, had a much more nuanced understanding of that claim, for he was not nationalistic as was the traditional Deuteronomic cohort. Had he been so, he would not have been appointed to the position of provincial governor or carry the outward signs of that his current office. If he were to respond positively to Haggai's promise it would inevitably involve him in betraying his Persian masters. Why was there no further word from Haggai, the editor or even from Zerubbabel as to what happened next? The editor clearly knew of the meeting but has remained silent as to the outcome. The editor has not reported anything other than what Haggai is said to have passed on to Zerubbabel. Readers may suggest that particular implications can be found in these highly emotive and distant promises addressed to the governor and find eschatological indications therein, but one needs to think carefully as to whether the meanings alleged are actually supported by the text itself or whether when reading another's 'mail', one has imported alien ideas and reached unsubstantiated conclusions.

On Being Chosen

One challenge that Haggai presents has to do with the belief that God has chosen one human community, and chosen to engage with it more intimately than with others (Hag. 2.23; Deut. 29.14-15). Haggai's theology was grounded in the belief that God had chosen the people of Israel and with them entered a covenantal relationship that was exclusive (see Deut. 4.5-8, 20; 7.1-8; 10.14-15). This was a fundamental notion rooted in the Mosaic covenant, and it became the single lens through which, from then on, the entire story of the people of Israel was viewed and re-told, including the earliest moments going back to the call of Abraham. The story of what became 'the people of Israel' cannot be understood or evaluated apart from this self-understanding.

Haggai absorbed and reveled in this belief, a view ingrained and sustained by Israel's annual festivals as well as within family gatherings (Deut. 6.20-25). While this may have been ancient Israel's empowering view of itself vis-à-vis Yahweh, it was nevertheless a claim that the Deuteronomic cohort in particular advanced for its own self-serving reasons. Believing oneself to be specially chosen by God was and is a very comforting notion. However, if one sees oneself as 'chosen', there is an obvious implication—it contrasts with those who are the 'non-chosen', the *gôyîm*, or the 'uncircumcised'. Under this rubric, 'the chosen' tend to view the 'non-chosen' as less significant than themselves; they could be 'shaken' and stripped, for Israel's sole benefit (Hag. 2.7-8). It is a view of the self as privileged that when taken seriously, as the Deuteronomic cohort did, alienates one from 'the other'. Despite the fact that the 'chosen' also saw themselves as servants of Yahweh, living by God's laws and conditions as set by the covenantal relationship, there was always a narrow tribal sense that alienated those who were not within the fold.

Allied with their belief in their having been chosen was the view that God had given them the land of Canaan to be their homeland in perpetuity, regardless of the fact that it was already inhabited by a variety of tribal groups. To assert their right to the land, the Israelites used the belief in their being a chosen people as justification for their attempt to destroy all the tribal groups currently occupying that land; this was presented as a divinely ordered policy of genocide (Deut. 4.38; 7.1-6). Even though the post-Exodus community was unable to drive out the 'squatters' (Judg. 1.19-35), the belief persisted, and continues to persist, that the Israelites were the legitimate and exclusive owners of that territory. For Haggai, this land was where their God Yahweh had determined to 'put his name', so his support for Temple rebuilding can be well understood.

'Chosenness' subsequently became one of the discriminating views that shaped the way in which the first-century CE community of Christ-followers saw themselves (e.g. 1 Pet. 1.2; 2.9). Although the Christian community did not adopt the Deuteronomic 'land' notion—they were too scattered to make that meaningful—nevertheless 'chosenness' became one of the continuing notions that would influence self-understanding in the early Christian communities. It is and remains a notion that tends to exclusive views of one's importance or privilege, the validity of one's ideas about God, but it is also a notion that is difficult to reconcile with a theology in which unconditional divine love is available for all, regardless of national or religious stripe. 'Chosenness' may give one a false sense of importance, of spiritual privilege tending to arrogance when confronted by difference, for Christian mission is often seen as requiring 'the other' to reject one's former identity in order to accept the Christian paradigm.

On God and Nature

A further challenge inherent in the worldview endorsed by Haggai is the belief that God not only 'strikes' the world with natural disasters such as pandemics, tsumanis, droughts, floods, forest fires and the like (Hag. 2.17), but more importantly, that God weaponizes the natural world as a means to punish a recalcitrant people. Disasters happen, be they naturally occurring or human derived. This is an inescapable fact. However, to link them directly to what one believes to be a divine act as intended punishment depends entirely on one's theological perspective.

Haggai's view of the divine purpose enacted via natural disasters or crises is clearly a contested notion, as Israel's Wisdom tradition noted (see Job and Ecclesiastes). The many crises that often afflict the world and its human and animal populations are real. Disasters that strike, such as earthquakes and tidal waves, pandemics or devastating bushfires resulting from lightning strikes, birth defects and more can so easily be attributed to divine activity but only if one assumes that this is the way the divine one, the creator, works. A simple biblical quote from Deuteronomy or elsewhere is not sufficient to justify or prove this assumption. However, if one wishes to adopt the point of view that Haggai has presented, then the fact that the impact of such disasters is totally indiscriminate for those, be they human, animal or insect, who are innocently swept up in those crises points to a God who is fickle and uncaring of those who suffer as a consequence.

One may accept the thesis that the God revealed in the Scriptures is the creator of the natural world and is in control, whether directly or indirectly. However, it is a rather large step from there to claim, and be able to demonstrate, that one specific natural event, such as a tsunami, is attributable to God's purposive action, and moreover to claim it as divine punishment for some imagined human evil. The nature of any relationship posited between God and the natural world is surely far more complex than the simple cause and effect that Haggai assumed and applied.

God and the Nations

An important element in Haggai's perspective on God was that, whether as creator or as warrior, God is viewed as active on the international political stage. While this is a perspective shared with other prophetic interpreters of world events, Haggai's particular presentation was of God intervening in the cut and thrust of world politics for the singular benefit of his chosen people. While other prophets such as Isaiah saw the divine hand in foreign attacks on Israel itself as disciplinary (Isa. 10.5-6), Haggai's view was more nationalistic. Despite the DH acknowledging God's hand in the fall of Judah and the subsequent exile of many to Babylon, Haggai believed the nations and their resources as God's to claim and to recover because of the covenantal arrangement God had with Israel. In this specific case, Haggai believed that his Jerusalem house would provide his God with glory and honour (1.8; 2.7-9). Something similar is also implied in the promise Haggai is said to have conveyed to Zerubbabel, that he would be elevated over all kingdoms and powers (2.20-23), leading to Judaea's anticipated mastery within the region.

Understanding world events in terms of God's intervention, as an expression of his plan and purpose, relies on an ideology such as that supported by Haggai. It is a worldview that is not restricted to ancient times, for even today some would claim that God was especially on their side, for 'In God we trust'. Like Constantine's shield emblazoned, it is said, with the cross and the words 'In this sign conquer', the idea that a belief in God or obedience to some divine directive will enhance one's own and the nation's interests can be found alive today. If one accepts the notion that God is intimately involved in the political arena, such involvement cannot be partisan unless one's view of God is limited and self-serving. During the World Wars of the past century combatants on both sides who were Christians prayed to the same God for help to defeat the other side, the enemy other. A simplistic notion that one's God has control of world powers and will intervene to aid or rescue one from the threats posed, especially if one holds the right beliefs, makes a mockery of religious commitment. A confession, a belief that God has power to control the fate of nations may be a thesis that some will endorse because it seems 'biblical', but many will find problematic in the specific application.

On Prophecy

I have noted the challenge when reading prophetic literature of determining whether a prophet's message derives from a claimed divine source or from a prophet's own personal insights and concerns. (See 'Prophetic Insight' in the **Introduction**.) The messenger form, within which the written messages of Haggai and others are placed, asserts that the words derive from an external revealed source (1.1), but a modern reader still is required to evaluate the claim that God is the source of that prophetic word. Was Haggai's reported challenge as to the Temple rebuilding a divinely sourced word, or did it derive primarily from his own deeply personal concern?

One key component of the prophetic role generally was that of alerting the individual or community to a specific situation or issuing a warning about an issue that needed addressing. Prophets also brought messages that might give hope, that could encourage and sustain. Those addressed were a prophet's immediate audience, a message concerning their present and, at times, their imminent future. The social or moral criticisms voiced by the prophets, regardless of its 'source', were clearly addressed to their contemporaries, as were the threatened punishments. The element of promise or threat that may accompany the prophet's message was usually expressed in hyperbolic language, and one has to admit—despite the danger of being charged a false prophet—that many of the prophetic messages were not fulfilled as delivered. This is a fact impinging on Haggai's presentation. How should his promises be understood?

Deuteronomy 18.14-22 speaks of the prophet and the criteria for establishing that a certain individual was or was not a genuine prophet. It was the fulfilment, the actualization of the prophetic word that allowed the community to recognize and affirm a prophet's *bona fides* and mission, and perhaps to take seriously what has been said. In Haggai's case, while he advocated the rebuilding of the Temple, there was an issue with his being regarded as a 'genuine' prophet unless it could be established that his promises about shaking the nations to have them release their treasures for the Temple's glorification were realized. We do not have a record of this happening during the four years it took to rebuild the Temple. For the prophets, there was always a practical difficulty in their being recognized as 'true' prophets—the audience had to wait many years before any evidence of 'fulfilment' was available—all were potentially false prophets until events or outcomes proved otherwise, and they then could be affirmed retroactively as genuine. Analyzing and explaining past or current situations was one thing; making promises about the future was quite another.

Were Haggai's promises to his audiences regarding the Temple/treasury giving them a false hope? Or were the audiences aware that what Haggai said was typical of prophetic exaggerated speech and so interpreted accordingly? Postponing or projecting Haggai's promises into some distant future, as some modern readers are wont to do, and suggesting some distant fulfilment may seem to minimize the problem of seemingly unfulfilled prophecies; but one might ask whether it is the 'promise' component of prophetic oracles that is their primary purpose or function? Surely the major goal of any prophetic message was to challenge contemporary society as to its manner of living, one that reflected its relationship with God, whether that challenge came allegedly from a divine source or from personal insights. Promises made using hyperbole may have given hope and encouraged an audience to expect a different future, but the hyperbole itself was a literary device that should not be read as literal fact.

Theological Exclusivism

There is also the tension noted between the prophet Haggai and the two leaders of the community, Zerubbabel and Joshua. While Haggai was what I have called a Deuteronomic 'hardliner', Zerubbabel and Joshua I consider to have been more open and accepting of difference, amenable to Persian ideas and policy. Without this broad view, neither Zerubbabel nor Joshua would have received his appointment from the Persian authorities. The tension between Haggai and the two leaders I have suggested arose from different personal responses to living within a foreign environment: Haggai, resistant to non-Jewish ideas, and the two leaders as amenable to them. Haggai's ideology was wooden and fixed; that of the leaders was open and flexible.

Immersion in the East Asian cultural worlds over a period of almost 30 years, requiring in-depth study of two major languages and cultures, has had a profound impact on my early self-awareness and my theological understanding; it has reshaped my basic religious perceptions. But one does not have to live in an alien culture for years in order to have a similar experience and perhaps come to this same realization. Many modern societies are no longer so monocultural that they can ignore the presence of other worldviews impinging on their own traditional model; our next-door immigrant neighbour may well challenge our old view of the world, our sense of self and narrow identity. Acknowledging this reality can open one to a non-exclusivist understanding of faith, a totally new understanding of what 'mission' can and should be in such a varied world, and the place of other ancient wisdom traditions as a bridge between different cultures and religions. Most importantly, openness to new perspectives gives freedom and a new depth to interpersonal relationships across cultures and religions.

Analogical Application

Despite the fact that there are some confronting issues for modern readers inherent in Haggai's basic message, finding analogies between the past and the present and seeking figurative application have been the most obvious ways of noting this document's ongoing relevance. This is especially so of the christological reading, or the New Testament 'goal', of the Haggai text of 2.20-23. That being said, there are those who retain a literal reading of Haggai, accepting without question the principles and conclusions that approximate those of Haggai and the Deuteronomists. So for them, yes, God does intervene in both the natural and the geopolitical worlds, and the faithful are able to discern 'rightly' what purpose(s) is served by each. To this group, the Covid-19 pandemic and the 9/11 Twin Towers attack in New York City can offer examples, analogies, of divine judgment against the human community; but the reason(s) suggested in justification of such claims depend on the personal concerns and ideology of the one making the claim—usually what that individual or cohort considers the most egregious of sins. Many, however, will find this analogy too subjective, too problematic to accept.

The fact that Haggai's focus was on a material building, the Temple, may be and has been read analogically to justify work on constructing a new religious building, and a building that is the best and most elaborate that a community can afford. Haggai's vision for a Temple and treasures that would glorify God and honour God can be read as support for plans to construct a massive church decorated with the finest art works and gold appointments. History is replete with such examples.

At another level, the mission of Haggai in the rebuilding of the Temple and community from 520 BCE may be seen as analogically relevant to the mission of church building and church planting in the modern era. More important than the growth in the number of churches, however, is the prophetic role, championing social and justice issues. Although Haggai showed no particular interest in other than the religious dimension, the sense of having a mission from God to advance the interests of all in the community is one definition of the church and its role today. Of course, a prophetic mission is not confined to the church, as there are many secular crusaders whose concern for the cosmos, for climate and for social-justice issues does not stem from any religious motivation or command, but simply from a deep human concern for the world and its people.

Analogical application of Haggai's concerns is dependent on the personal proclivities of the one making the analogy and so is usually highly subjective. Haggai applied the priests' advice in 2.10-13 analogically to his people, though the grounds for such application remain opaque, mysterious, unexplained, hidden from modern readers. It is a warning to modern pastors and preachers to be cautious about using the analogical method when interpreting or applying ancient Scripture not originally intended for a modern audience, to avoid superficial analogies and questionable comparisons.

Conclusion

I began this exploration of Haggai conscious of the 'danger' of importing alien ideas and values into my reading plan. Whether I have been able to avoid or even to minimize the 'danger' and read the editor's text from a perspective that allowed the several facets of his report to be critically but sympathetically revealed is for the reader to determine. My earnest hope is that I have been able to highlight from the text the main ideas advanced by the prophet and those who kept alive evidence of his mission in the context of their lived experience in Judaea of 520 BCE. It has to do with Haggai's place in the theological development of the people of Israel in the postexilic period.

What cannot be disputed is that Haggai was deeply rooted in the theology or ideology of the Deuteronomic cohort. That cohort represented what was one of the most significant theological paradigms in ancient Israel, by retelling the national story, beginning with the forefathers and on into the travails of the exilic and postexilic communities, in light of the Exodus tradition. While enormously significant, readers of the Old Testament should not be misled by the sheer volume of material that reflects the Deuteronomic perspective from which so much of its content has been written. The Deuteronomic paradigm and its language must be seen in context as one available paradigm, and not read as the only or universally acceptable ideology; it must not be absolutized. My reading has sought to distinguish between Haggai as an exemplar of the convinced Deuteronomist, and Zerubbabel and Joshua on the other hand, whose broader view was a legitimate alternative. Although the text does not reveal what their theological position was in any detail, the fact that they viewed matters differently from Haggai is indisputable, and that difference must be honoured, for all theologies are limited and inadequate.

In addition, I have made several references to the fact that co-existing with Deuteronomy and related material was the wisdom tradition, especially as seen in Job and Qoheleth. These latter books take issue with the viewpoint of the Deuteronomists. Their authors work from a very different perspective, concluding that the viewpoint and conclusions of Deuteronomy are too simplistic; human experience is far more complicated than that represented by Haggai's simplistic explanation of the crisis facing Judaeans in 520 BCE as divine punishment. The theological landscape in 520 BCE was therefore more complex, with competing interpretations and visions based on differing sources of reflection or inspiration. As a result, to read Haggai as though it represented the only and 'correct' view of God and of the way in which God interacts with his people is a false reading, or a biased reading that ignores the reality of competing theological positions. Giving preference to the prophetic word and mission over that of the sage or priest because that prophetic word is formally classified as 'the word of the Lord' reflects a reading plan that is questionable; it requires more careful consideration of the set phrase and its use.

As for Haggai, I have concluded that the editor's report of his messages and promises, while valuable as representing the perspective of one cohort of the period, leaves much space for a more qualified and nuanced evaluation of his brief mission and its effectiveness.

Appendix A

Haggai and Prophetic Forms

One of the striking features of Haggai is its narrative form; other traditional prophetic forms are not found. However, its application of the one form that can be linked with prophetic oracles, namely, the messenger form, '*Thus says the Lord (of hosts) . . . says the Lord*', that traditionally opens and closes prophetic oracles, is used in such an unconventional manner that it suggests that the final editor of Haggai either was not very familiar with the form or chose to modify it and use it in his own personal manner, as an emphatic.

Each of the dated messages begins with a narrative introduction: 'The word of the Lord came to/by the hand of Haggai the prophet . . .' (1.1, 3; 2.1, 10, 20). There are then within each day's report some quoted material that begins with the initial element of the traditional messenger form, '*Thus says the Lord of hosts*'—*koh 'āmar yhwh ṣᵉbā'ôt* (1.2, 5, 7; 2.6, 11). It is noticeable that the opening element of the form is used only on these five occasions. It is the closing element of the form that predominates: 1.8, 9c, 13; 2.4a, 4c, 4d, 7d, 8b, 9b, 9d, 14c, 17d, 23a, 23b, 23c. Furthermore, the closing form appears as either *nᵉ'um yhwh* or *'āmar yhwh*. What should be noted is that the two sections in which the focus is on 'shaking' the cosmos and nations are the two locations where the concluding phrases are concentrated—2.6-9 and 2.21-23—it is almost as though it is a deliberate choice by the editor to insert multiple examples of the concluding form in order to support and emphasize the theme. They do not signal the close of a subject or speech, for there is no observable correlation between the opening component '*Thus says the Lord*' and what should normally complete each individual oracle.

Added to this is the varied expression used in the concluding phrases: not all follow the Hebrew *nᵉ'um yhwh (ṣᵉbā'ôt)* form; the editor has also used *'āmar yhwh (ṣᵉbā'ôt)*, giving a total of four different versions of the concluding marker. In such a short document, the numerous examples (15 in all) of this varied conclusion suggest that the editor departed from the normal application of the form, creating his own versions and employed them as a means of emphasis, a way to underline the specific point he is trying to make. In 2.23, for example, the editor places the phrase after 'on that day' after 'I will take you' and after 'I have chosen you', each being a brief and independent statement that is thus highlighted. It does not serve primarily as a concluding marker.

The fact that the formal convention is applied in a non-standard manner, without attention to basic principles should prevent overzealous interpretation of the closing form's significance, especially in terms of marking its source as a divine word.

Select Bibliography

Books

Aharoni, Y., M. Avi-Yonah, A.F. Rainey and Z. Safrai, *The Carta Bible Atlas* (Jerusalem: Carta, 4th edn, 1968–2002).
Barker, J.R., *Disputed Temple: A Rhetorical Analysis of the Book of Haggai* (Minneapolis, MN: Fortress Press, 2017).
Clark, D.J., and H.A. Hatton, *A Handbook on Haggai* (UBS Handbook Series; New York: UBS, 2002).
Finkelstein, I., and N.A. Silberman, *The Bible Unearthed* (New York: Simon & Schuster, 2001).
Jacobs, M.R., *The Books of Haggai and Malachi* (Grand Rapids, MI: Eerdmans, 2017).
Meadowcroft, T., *Haggai* (Readings: A New Biblical Commentary; Sheffield: Sheffield Phoenix Press, 2006).
Myers, C., and E.M. Myers, *Haggai, Zechariah 1–8* (AB, 25B; New Haven, CT; Doubleday, 1987).
Petersen, D.L., *Haggai and Zechariah 1–8: A Commentary* (OTL; Philadelphia: Fortress Press, 1984).
Redditt, P.L., *Haggai, Zechariah, and Malachi* (NCBC; Grand Rapids, MI: Eerdmans, 1995).
Smith, R.L., *Micah–Malachi* (WBC, 32; Dallas, TX: Word Books, 1984).
Sweeney, M.A., *The Twelve Prophets* (Berit Olam, 2; Collegeville, MN: Liturgical Press, 2000).
Verhoef, P.A., *The Books of Haggai and Malachi* (NICOT; Grand Rapids, MI: Eerdmans, 1987).
Wolff, H.W., *Haggai: A Commentary* (trans. M. Kohl; Minneapolis, MN: Augsburg, 1988).

Articles

Assis, Eli, 'A Disputed Temple (Haggai 2.1-9)', *ZAW* (2007), pp. 582-96.
Clark, D.J., 'Problems in Haggai 2.15-19', *BT* 1 (1983), pp. 432-39.
— 'Discourse Structure in Haggai', *JOTT* 5 (1992), pp. 13-24.
Clines, D.J.A., 'Haggai's Temple, Constructed, Deconstructed and Reconstructed', in D.J.A. Clines, *Interested Parties* (Sheffield: Sheffield Phoenix Press, 2009), pp. 46-75.
Ogden, G.S., 'A Case Study for Study Bibles: The Book of Haggai', *BT* 69 (2018), pp. 176-83.

www.ingramcontent.com/pod-product-compliance
Lightning Source LLC
Chambersburg PA
CBHW072155160426
43197CB00012B/2390